Scottish Love Poems

Scottish Love Poems

A Personal Anthology
Antonia Fraser

CANONGATE

EDINBURGH

First published in 1975 by Canongate Publishing Limited
17 Jeffrey Street, Edinburgh

Reprinted by Penguin Books in 1976
Reissued by Canongate Publishing 1988

Introduction © Antonia Fraser 1975

ISBN 0 86241 167 X

Book designed by Ruari McLean
Drawings by James Hutcheson
Printed and bound in Great Britain
by Butler and Tanner, Frome, Somerset

for Stephanie – Then and Now
With love.

Acknowledgements

In assembling this anthology I was much helped by friends who love poetry, friends who love Scotland, and best of all, those who love both. It would be invidious to single out names, many of which feature on the following pages. However, I would particularly like to thank Carolyn Proctor for her researches, Charles Wild of Canongate Publishing, my daughter Flora Fraser, and Mrs Patsy Parsons for her typing. Above all, I am grateful to Stephanie and Angus Wolfe Murray but for whose enterprise there would have been no assembly in the first place.

Antonia Fraser

For permission to reprint the poems in this anthology acknowledgement is made to the following:

for 'The Point of Love', by Alan Bold, from *A Perpetual Motion Machine*, to Chatto and Windus Ltd. and the Wesleyan University Press, Middleton, Connecticut; for 'Country Girl', by George Mackay Brown, from *The Year of the Whale*, to the Hogarth Press Ltd.; for 'Fiddler's Song' and for the extract from 'Lord of the Mirrors', by George Mackay Brown, from *Poems New and Selected*, to the Hogarth Press Ltd. and Harcourt Brace Jovanovich Inc., New York; for 'Wedding', by George Mackay Brown, to the author; for 'Three Love Poems for My Wife', by George Bruce, from *Collected Poems*, to the Edinburgh University Press; for 'Shepherdess', from *Collected Poems*, to the literary estate of the late Norman Cameron and the Hogarth Press Ltd.; for 'Duo', by William Keys, from *Scottish Poetry 3*, for 'Floating off to Timor', by Edwin Morgan, and the two poems by Pete Morgan, from *Scottish Poetry 4*, for 'And Our Gifts to the Seasons', by Thomas Clark, 'The Straits', by Valerie Gillies, 'Words, for E', by Tom Leonard, 'Young Girl', by Menzies McKillop, 'Question and Answer', by Alasdair Maclean, and the two poems by Robert Tait, all from *Scottish Poetry 5,* and for 'The Gentle Ambush', by George Macadam, 'Diane', by Stewart McIntosh, and 'At Kilbryde Castle', by Lorn M. Macintyre, all from *Scottish Poetry 6,* to the authors and to the Edinburgh University Press; for 'Arrivals 1', by Stewart Conn, and the two poems by Tom McGrath, to the editor of *Aquarius;* for 'Thread', by Catherine Lucy Czerkawska, and 'Marry the Lass?', by Andrew Greig, both from *White Boats,* to the authors and to Garret Arts; for 'There Was a Sang', by Helen B. Cruickshank, to the author and to Reprographia; for 'Black Tomintoul', by Ian Hamilton Finlay, from *The Dancers Inherit the Party* (Migrant Press, 1960), to the author; for 'Christmas Letter Home', by G. S. Fraser, to the author; for 'Between Appointments', by Giles Gordon, first published by the Sceptre Press, and for 'A Former Love', first published in the *Scotsman,* to the author; for 'The Grave of Love', by the late Sir Alexander Gray, to Mr John Gray; for the two poems by J. F. Hendry, to the author; for 'Tam i' the Kirk', to Curtis Brown Ltd. on behalf of the estate of the late Violet Jacob; for the two poems by Morley Jamieson, both first published in the *Scotsman,* to the author; for 'Love Poem 3', by Laughton Johnston, first published in *Akros 24,* to the author; for 'A Ballad of Orpheus', by Maurice Lindsay, from *Selected Poems 1942–72,* published by Robert Hale Ltd., to the author; for 'Today', by Liz Lochhead, first published in *Akros 25,* to the author; for 'A Song for an Able Bastard', by the late Eric Linklater, from *A Dragon Laughed,* to Jonathan Cape Ltd., and for 'A Memory, Now Distant', to Mrs Eric Linklater; for 'Near Midnight', by Norman MacCaig, from *Surroundings,* to the Hogarth Press Ltd. and the Wesleyan University Press Inc., Middleton, Connecticut; for 'Poem for a Goodbye', from *The Sinai Sort,* and for 'You Went Away', from *Riding Lights,* both by Norman MacCaig, to the Hogarth Press Ltd.; for 'Bridal Day', by the late Sir Compton Mackenzie, to Lady Mackenzie; for Iain Crichton Smith's translations from the Gaelic of Sorley Maclean, from *Poems to Eimhir,* to Northern House and Victor Gollancz Ltd. and to Mr Smith and Dr Maclean; for 'For Bonny Elspeth', by Hamish Macbride, to Mr James Michie; for 'Sang', by Robert McLellan, first published in *Poetry Scotland,* to the author and to William MacLellan, Publishers; for 'Love Song', by Joseph Macleod, to the author; for the two poems by Robert Nye, to the author; for 'Less than Love', by Aileen Campbell Nye, to the author; for 'I Saw the Light Yesterday', by Galina Ogilvie-Laing, to the author; for the three poems by Alastair Reid, to the author; for 'The Circle', by Alan Riddell, from *The Stopped Landscape,* to the author and to Hutchinson and Co. Ltd.; for 'To My Mountain', from *The Collected Poems of Kathleen Raine,* © 1956 Kathleen Raine, to the author and to

Hamish Hamilton Ltd.; for 'Continent o Venus', by Alexander Scott, to the author and to Akros Publications; for 'To X', by Tom Scott, to the author; for 'The Shadows' and 'Tonight', by Iain Crichton Smith, from *Poems for Donalda*, published by Ulsterman Publications, Belfast, and for 'Farewell', to the author; for 'The Mandrake Hairt', 'Wuidreek', and 'We Shall Never Want', to the late Sydney Goodsir Smith, and for 'There is a Tide', also by Sydney Goodsir Smith, to Southside Ltd.; for the three poems by William Soutar and the sonnet by Mark Alexander Boyd, to the Trustees of the National Library of Scotland; for 'To Anybody at All', by Margaret Tait, from *Origins and Elements*, to the author; for the two poems by W. Price Turner, to the author; for the two poems by Ruthven Todd, to William MacLellan, Publishers; for 'The Shepherd's Dochter', to the estate of the late Douglas Young; for 'Love Charm', *from Carmina Gadelica* vol. II, to the Scottish Academic Press, Ltd. and to the trustees of the late Professor J. C. Watson; for 'The Dart of Love', 'Love' and 'The Trout of the Well', translated by G. R. D. McLean, from *Poems of the Western Highlanders*, to the Society for Promoting Christian Knowledge; for the translation 'I Gave You My Love', to Professor Derick Thomson; for the translation 'Alas for Him Whose Sickness is Love', to the Scottish Academic Press Ltd. and the Scottish Gaelic Texts Society.

The seven poems by Hugh MacDiarmid reprinted with permission of Macmillan Publishing Co. Inc., from *The Collected Poems of Hugh MacDiarmid*, copyright © 1948, 1962 by Christopher Murray Grieve; the three poems by Edwin Muir, from *Collected Poems*, reprinted by permission of Faber and Faber Ltd. and the Oxford University Press Inc., New York; 'From the Night-Window', by Douglas Dunn, from *Terry Street*, reprinted by permission of Faber and Faber Ltd. and the Chilmark Press Inc., New York; 'Mary's Song', from *The Turn of the Day*, and 'Anemones', both by the late Marion Angus, reprinted by permission of Faber and Faber Ltd.; 'The Shell', from *Collected Poems 1958-70*, and 'Poem Before Birth', from *Shrapnel and a Poet's Year*, both by George MacBeth, reprinted by permission of Macmillan, London and Basingstoke, and Atheneum Publishers, New York; 'A Letter', by Burns Singer, © Marie Battle Singer, from *Collected Poems*, Carcanet Press Ltd.

Every attempt has been made to contact copyright holders, but if any material has been included for which permission has not been sought, apologies are tendered in advance to proprietors and publishers concerned.

Contents

ix

Romantics

Unromantics

Marriages

The Nature of Love

Obsessions

Warnings

Laments

Unrequited Love

Fainthearts

Doomed Love

Farewells

Love Lost

Love in Abeyance

Introduction

The purpose of this anthology is first and foremost to give pleasure. It has a secondary intention: to demonstrate the romantic richness of Scottish love poetry down the ages to the present day. But since it is in no sense an academic work, either by design or execution, its primary purpose remains that of giving pleasure rather than instruction. It will be found that poems have been chosen entirely on grounds of personal predilection – mine. I have made no attempt to 'represent' any given poet, let alone include a poem out of dutiful respect for its excellence, if that excellence has not appealed to me. The omissions therefore can be taken to be deliberate. Because I have chosen all the poems for the sake of the emotions they have aroused in my own breast, it can be assumed that the old favourites which are missing, have been ignored because although they may be old, they are not my favourites.

As to the arrangement, this is neither chronological nor alphabetical but in categories – I should like to call them the categories of love if that did not sound too rigorous. In fact the categories are more impressionistic than the word itself suggests. Nevertheless I did not want to rob the reader altogether of a sense of time. After all, if one loves particular verses, it is relevant to interest if not appreciation whether the author is fifteenth-century or alive at the present moment. The names of Scottish poets, incidentally, have an admirable continuity which means that there is absolutely no way of telling from them alone – how splendidly numerous for example the Scotts are, and there are actually two Alexander

Scotts in this volume, one sixteenth-century and one writing today. In the end it seemed to me that the best and least obtrusive way of feeding this interest was to give each poet's dates within the text itself. In this way it was hoped to preserve a sense of choice without cutting off the reader altogether from the background of Scottish literature.

Naturally all anthologies, however eclectically titled, contain an element of the personal, since the mere act of selection implies some kind of choice or other. But in my own life, I have derived most pleasure from three anthologies which were deliberately personal – three tried travelling companions. Palgrave's *Golden Treasury* was the first book of poetry I owned, a copy still lovingly preserved. Then there was Maurice Baring's *Have you Anything to Declare?*, translated from many languages, and the ideal bedside book. Thirdly I would name *God of a Hundred Names*, prayers of many peoples and creeds, of which Victor Gollancz wrote in his foreword that 'if any, whatever their religion or formal lack of it ... should find here a useful source book for prayer or meditation, particularly before or after sleep, we should be happy'. Having discovered in it myself, particularly in time of grief, a great solace, I should like to think that the present volume would, in its turn, be a useful source book for those in love. That it might be read with enjoyment by those happily in love, that it might comfort those in distress through the unhappiness of love, that it might be presented by lovers to each other, all this would fulfil my hopes for this particular anthology.

Why then restrict the catchment area to Scottish love poets? The explanation is rooted once again in personal predilection. In the course of historical researches into sixteenth-century Scotland for the very different purpose of biography, I was struck by the wealth and passion of the poetry of the period. Alexander Montgomerie, for example, captured my heart with his lines to his mistress:

So swete a kis yistrene fra thee I reft,
In bowing down thy body on the bed,
That evin my lyfe within thy lippis I left ...

It is with his verse 'Evin dead behold I breathe' with which this book fittingly ends. Poetry is also much entwined around the family tree of the Scottish monarchy, the subjects of these historical studies. Among poems included are an extract from the courtly 'Kingis Quair' of James I, and his 'Sang on Absence' (possibly not by his own hand but at least one authority attributes it to him and I have allowed him the royal benefit of the doubt). Then there is the melancholy little French song of Mary Queen of Scots on the death of Francis I and the poetry of her son King James VI, in which one detects genuine poignancy, be it the cry of despair for the banished loved one Esmé Stuart, his Phoenix, or his expostulation on the enduring nature of love. As for Mary's second husband and James' father, Lord Darnley, he himself was no mean poet, as evinced by his graceful lines of lament 'If langour makis men licht'.

History apart, I have always rated Burns the Scot and Byron the Scot too – a remark which sometimes raises English eyebrows, but of course George Gordon was of Scottish origins as he himself acknowledged – among my two favourite love poets in any language. My unequivocal adoration of Burns, what Tennyson called 'his exquisite songs ... in shape each of them has the perfection of the berry; in the light the radiance of the dewdrop', will be obvious to the reader. It is the sheer range of moods of love which he expresses which astonish one in an anthology of this nature: there was scarcely a category in which one of his poems could not have figured, summing it all up. Then there is my life-long passion for Sir Walter Scott (who after all began his career as a poet not a novelist), to say nothing of appreciation for the new as well as the old, Hugh MacDiarmid and George

Mackay Brown for example, which existed long before this anthology was ever mooted. As one once married to a Scot when we lived a proportion of the year in Scotland, I have always been a convinced believer in Romantic Scotland rather than Caledonia Stern and Wild. Nor is this belief a mere illusion. Investigation among the younger Scottish poets, apart from the long loved favourites, has amply demonstrated its continued existence. Out of the one hundred and eighty odd poems here chosen, nearly half emerge out of the twentieth century, and a high proportion of these are the work of living – and young – poets. Ireland, it has sometimes seemed to me as one of Irish extraction, has an unfairly inflated reputation as a cradle of poetry, and Scotland a deflated one. In short, then, and let me not deny it, I have always been totally and happily prejudiced in favour of Scottish poetry.

In defence of my prejudice it is only fair to point out that many excellent anthologies, of a deliberately representative nature, exist, for which this is not intended in any way to be a substitute. Notably there is the *Oxford Book of Scottish Verse*, chosen by John MacQueen and Tom Scott; concentrating on newer works, one might single out *Modern Scottish Poetry*, edited by Maurice Lindsay, and *Contemporary Scottish Verse*, covering the decade 1959–1969, edited by Norman MacCaig and Alexander Scott. To go further back, there is *Ballatis of Luve*, also edited by John MacQueen, exposing the treasure house of courtly poetry in the sixteenth century. To these, and to others, including the many vigorous modern offshoots such as the admirable *Scottish Poetry* series, 1–6, edited by George Bruce, Maurice Lindsay and Edwin Morgan for the Edinburgh University Press, it is to be hoped that readers may turn for a fuller picture, their curiosity aroused by toying with the present volume.

It is true that having read so much Scottish poetry in this good cause, I have come to the conclusion that the strongest passion of all in the Scottish breast is for Scotland itself.

Deliberately, believing that would be an anthology on its own, I have ignored that kind of love, the patriotic love of country, in favour of love between human beings. I have therefore restrained myself from quoting such favourite lines as those of Douglas Young on the old Highlands –

> That old lonely lovely way of living
> In Highland places – twenty years a-growing,
> Twenty years flowering, twenty years declining ...

Such a poem, it seems to me, together with very many poems about the Scottish heart, be it in the Highlands or the Lowlands, belong properly to another selection. Beyond that there have been no intentional restrictions – Hugh MacDiarmid's famous 'Empty Vessel' concerns the love of a mother for her baby, George MacBeth's 'The Shell' describes love for a lost mother, and G. S. Fraser's letter to a sister is self-explanatory – even if Eros has tended to predominate.

Otherwise I have ranged as widely as possible. John Buchan, in his own delightful personal anthology *The Northern Muse* ('It contains the things which, as a lover of Scots verse, I turn to most often and desire to have in a compact form'), described himself as using the ballads sparingly because they were accessible in many editions: but I have not felt held back by their popularity. It was however mildly surprising to discover that they did not all, as was my first instinct to suppose, fall into the category of DOOMED LOVE. In fact the more one reads the ballads, from whatever age they emanate and whoever may have been their original inspiration, the more one is struck by the highly sophisticated and varied views of love which they propound. One is reminded of Hugh MacDiarmid's description of them as 'the journalism o' their day' –

> Yet a' at aince they soar up frae doggerel
> To heichts that only sheer genius scales.

Like great journalists, the ballad-makers covered love in all its different aspects – 'Earl Richard' here figures in UN-REQUITED LOVE, 'Lady Isabel and the Elf-Knight' belongs to the UNROMANTICS, and 'The Unquiet Grave', with its note of admonition to those who grieve too self-indulgently, to WARNINGS. 'The Baffled Knight' is clearly one of nature's FAINTHEARTS.

Nor for that matter have I attempted to delve into the problem of songs versus poems. As far as I am concerned, the two are inextricably entangled in much of Scottish poetry; but songs are included on the basis of words alone. It will be seen for example that the words of 'The Flowers of the Forest' find a place. This is not a tribute to the music, veiled, but simply because from the moment I first heard them, I coveted the words themselves.

One problem had to be faced squarely, and that was the problem of the Scots language. I am well aware that because I find some early Scots comprehensible (having been obliged to study it in the course of historical research) this does not necessarily apply to the rest of the English-reading public, including many native Scots. It is useless to ignore the difficulty, the very real difficulty, which this constitutes. R. L. Stevenson put it well in his Introduction to his own *Poems* of 1906 when he observed that although the Scots tongue had 'an authography of its own, lacking neither "authority nor author" … yet the temptation is great to lend a little guidance to the bewildered Englishman'. To this temptation I very nearly succumbed. With my aforesaid missionary feeling concerning early Scottish poetry, their sentiments so lyrical and contemporary if only the language barrier could be o'erleapt, I did toy momentarily with the idea of literally translating the more obscure verse. This would indeed have been a desperate remedy. As Stevenson continued: 'Some simple phonetic artifice might defend your verses from barbarous mishandling and yet not injure any

vested interests. So it seems at first, but there are rocks ahead.'
On these rocks, my scheme finally foundered. The lines have
their own balance, rhythm and metre, and as one kind friend
pointed out (who happened to possess both), to do the job
well, one would need the combined arts of the poet and the
translator. The time-honoured expedient of translating
certain highly obscure words as footnotes has therefore been
preferred: this in its turn has seemed more convenient for the
reader than a glossary at the back of the book.

I have, however, made two concessions: with the precedent
of Tom Scott's edition of the *Penguin Book of Scottish Verse*
to guide me, I have altered the confusing Early and Middle
Scots 'quh' to 'wh' and myself altered 'Gif' to 'If'. As a
result, I trust that English readers will be suitably encouraged
to persevere. In order that they may not simply skip the
earlier poems – which is their right, considering my avowed
aim of promoting enjoyment, but would be ultimately
regrettable – I take the liberty of recommending reading
them aloud. In one sense, all poetry should be read aloud,
and a poem which cannot be bettered by being read aloud, is a
dubious repository of the muse. But in another sense, it is by
reading aloud such poems as Dunbar's 'To a Ladye' that the
code of the unfamiliar terms may most easily be broken.

Gaelic on the other hand I have been compelled to pass by
(although not necessarily translations from it) because not
having it myself, it would be an affectation on my part to
include poems in that language, whose relative merits I am
not qualified to judge. The criterion for the translations has
for the same reason been poetic quality in their own right:
thus Iain Crichton Smith's interpretations of the Gaelic of
Sorley Maclean find a place, because they are manifestly
poetry. Sorley Maclean's own translations on the other hand
are not included since in a Preface to *Lines Review*, the
author has stated that these are simply prose renderings and
'in no sense to be regarded as poetry'. A translation by John

Sobieski Stuart, the nineteenth-century pretender and student of Highland lore, owes, one suspects, more to his own enterprise than to the original Gaelic and is therefore included. As for James Macpherson and *Ossian*, it seemed logical as well as desirable to embrace an extract of this splendid emanation of the romantic Scottish spirit, and prose or poetry, forgery and all, I would not have Selma's lamentations missing from my collection.

Let us now turn to the categories themselves. It should be pointed out that, superficially at least, these were suggested by the poems rather than the other way about. (Of course they do form part of the essentially personal nature of the work, and a psychoanalyst might perhaps learn something from them, even if nothing so self-revelatory was intended.) Be that as it may, my method was first of all to select all my most beloved poems and then arrange them into their natural categories, as might seem to be suggested by the material. Obviously one would expect one's own obsessions to emerge – WAITING and OLD LOVES are two of them – as indeed they emerge in the original choice of works. But as with abstract painting and still more with music, many different meanings can be read into the same haunting poem. It is possible, even likely, that some living poets will wonder in amazement at the category of poem in which they find their offspring being fostered. I can only express the hope in return that their surprise will be palliated by the knowledge that their poem was at least lavishly appreciated – otherwise it would not be included in the first place. Perhaps the surprised creator may be solaced by the thought that it is surely better to be loved and misunderstood than never to be loved at all.

The book seems to fall naturally into two parts, which may be described as the light and dark side of love. CELEBRATIONS presents those poems which are in themselves the quintessence of love poetry and need no further gloss: for although love, like the truth, is in real life rarely pure and never simple, in poetry at least it sometimes can be both. This section begins fitly with the greatest Scottish love poem of all, 'My luve is like a red, red rose,' although Hugh MacDiarmid's opening lines can hold their own in its company:

> My love is to the light of lights
> As a gold fawn to the sun ...

WOOINGS proved a particularly fertile field, to the extent that I formed the impression that there is something temperamentally dashing in the Scottish nature which enjoys the ardour of the chase, as Young Lochinvar might be described as a typical Scottish folk hero.

ENCOUNTERS ranges from William Keys' brilliantly cynical 'Duo' to Edwin Morgan's subtly disquieting lyric 'In Glasgow': in many if not all of the poems in this category, it seems to me, that sex is present in some form, sex, even if denied, despised or even suspected as in Ian Hamilton Finlay's offbeat 'Black Tomintoul'. It is present explicitly in Pete Morgan's 'The White Stallion': then there is Burns' forever ambivalent 'Comin' Thro' the Rye' (exactly what *did* go on?) and even Maggie Lauder's blithe encounter with the piper is not free from possibilities. It is left to Alastair Reid's 'At First Sight' to commemorate one aspect of a love affair which will survive as long as love itself does, the memory of the fatal impact.

ROMANTICS enshrines that side of the Scottish nature, sometimes denied by its critics, but for me summed up by the last line of Kathleen Raine's rightly famous 'To My Mountain':

> and oh, the sweet scent, and purple skies!

What makes certain of these poems ROMANTIC to me, where others, seemingly similar, belonged to CELEBRATIONS? The quality I sought here was a kind of purity of longing. John Buchan, in his Introduction to *The Northern Muse*, perceived a kind of dichotomy here: 'Romance in the North has always some salt of the pedestrian,' he wrote, 'and the most prosaic house of life has casements opening upon fairy seas.' But I found differently. A clear and limpid stream of romance runs through Scottish poetry right down to the present day. The modern romantics are not without their fantasies, strictly of their own time, as in W. Price Turner's 'Personal Column'; yet the poems of Lorn M. Macintyre and Valerie Gillies reveal the self-perpetuating strength of this category today. Whereas LAMENTS did tend to belong more to the past, and THE NATURE OF LOVE more to the present, ROMANTICS in Scotland are eternal.

As for the UNROMANTICS they are not necessarily modern. Sir Walter Scott's Nora is unromantic (if practical) in succumbing to the Earlie's son, just as much as Burns' more obvious hero who rates 'the nice yellow guineas' higher than the physical charms of a lass, and Eric Linklater's amiable bastard. With MARRIAGES, one reaches the culmination of the bright side of love – for all these poems are in some sense to do with consummation, even if not every one has the classical happy ending of these lines from the Western Highlands:

> The clouds flew over the mountain crest,
>   The spray was flecking the sea,
> She drew him close to her throbbing breast,
>   Her prisoner for aye to be,
> They went to kirk an it came the day ...

George Mackay Brown's 'Wedding' has, to say the least of it, a speculative ending, and Douglas Dunn's 'From the Night-Window', in which 'the sleepless, smoking in the dark ... count the years of their marriages', although finding a place in the same category as Allan Ramsay's 'The Generous Gentleman', is clearly describing a state several years further on.

From WARNINGS onwards starts the descent into the shadows: it is James Hogg, the Ettrick Shepherd's ominous Song from 'The Queen's Wake' which turned the young Mary Stuart pale. OBSESSIONS, too, belong to the dark side of love, be they Violet Jacob's compulsive 'Tam i' the Kirk' ('He canna sing for the sang that his ain he'rt raises') or the extract from *The Buik of Alexander* four hundred years earlier, which explains the total involvement with the loved one's physical appearance so common to passion. It is however Alexander Gray's translation from Heine which expresses the best fate for unhappy obsessions, the mighty coffin destined for a mighty grave in which should be laid:

> The auld sangs soored and cankered,
> Ill dreams that keep me fleyed ...
> It's my love I mean to lay there,
> And the dule I've tholed so lang.

UNREQUITED LOVE is more of an examination of the condition, that state of mind perhaps best summed up by two succinct lines taken from Scott's 'Lord of the Isles':

> No! sum thine Edith's wretched lot
> In these brief words. He loves her not.

although the sixteenth-century Alexander Scott might rival Sir Walter for terse good sense with his opening line: 'To luve unluvit it is a pane'. FAINTHEARTS on the other hand roughly speaking deserve what they get – even Stewart McIntosh's hitch-hiker who fails to give his girl driver a kiss is fairly in the same category as the anonymous author of 1500 who wrote: 'I luve, bot I dar nocht assay'. The final end of this desolation is LOVE LOST where once again

Burns says it all and says it best with 'Ae Fond Kiss'; yet even here Andrew Lang can express one salient and consoling point about lost loves:

> Who wins his love shall lose her,
>   Who loses her shall gain ...
> He loses her who gains her,
>   Who watches day by day,
> The dust of time that stains her,
>   The griefs that leave her gray ...

Now the mood changes to the numerous and insoluble mysteries which lie at the heart of the whole matter. L O V E IN ABEYANCE is intended to convey that curious aspect of love, too well known to all the amorously inclined, that those who are without its pangs often secretly regret them, so that many lovers are torn between desiring love and fearing it. The respite was given its most celebrated expression by Byron ('And the heart must pause to breathe, And love itself have rest'), but Liz Lochhead too ('but oh – oh insomniac moonlight') gives an evocative one-line description of the feelings which haunt the parted. And into this category also I have put William Soutar's description of that moment when sleep divides us all off, and the waking lover at least fears that love may be in abeyance:

> Through what quiet continents of your own
> Are you now walking, and with whom for a friend?

CHANGE AND PARADOX is another ambivalent category, the change and decay at the heart of love, often carried with it and endemic in the very closeness of the relationship, Laughton Johnston's fear 'that we may be becoming too familiar strangers'.

After that comes the levelling note of nostalgia – O L D LOVES: its theme is set in the romantic sense by Giles Gordon's 'A Former Love' and its conclusion with the faint disquiet that such encounters bring. But already with Burns' dedication of his poems to an early sweetheart, 'Once fondly lov'd, and still remember'd dear' – serenity creeps in. With ENDURING LOVE serenity is total.

One question will inevitably be raised in the reader's mind at the end of all this, as indeed it was raised in my mind at the very beginning: what is a Scot? There is no easy answer to this question, as to many of the most intriguing questions concerning our British society. For this reason, I have been guided by such yardsticks as the *Oxford Book of Scottish Verse* in the case of the dead. May their shades not haunt me, if I have unwittingly offended and been too ruthless in my captures. But with the living I have deliberately chosen Scots not only by birth but by adoption. Indeed, I have been prejudiced in favour of residence and inclination as well as strict blood, since it seems to me that in contrast to their well-known reputation for expatriatism, the Scots have also been invigorated by those who have joined their ranks. It would probably have been impossible to confine this anthology to those of Scottish racial purity with any degree of certainty: but in any case racial purity is not a concept of which I approve as a foundation for patriotism, believing passionately in hybridisation as a source of national strength.

I am sometimes reminded of the words of Gertrude Stein who on her deathbed enquired: 'What is the answer?' and when there was no reply, came back with 'What is the question, then?' It all depends what you mean by a Scot. I am inclined to the view, if it be not too Stein-like, that a Scot, like life, is what you make it, and certainly in the case of individuals, each one must be the judge of their own cause. To feel Scottish, as far as I am concerned, is to *be* Scottish.

Antonia Fraser

Celebrations of Love

A Red, Red Rose

O my luve is like a red, red rose
    That's newly sprung in June.
O, my luve is like the melodie,
    That's sweetly play'd in tune.

As fair art thou, my bonnie lass,
    So deep in luve am I,
And I will luve thee still, my dear,
    Till a' the seas gang dry.

Till a' the seas gang dry, my dear,
    And the rocks melt wi' the sun!
And I will love thee still, my dear,
    While the sands o' life shall run.

And fare thee weel, my only luve,
    And fare thee weel a while!
And I will come again, my luve,
    Tho it were ten thousand mile!

Robert Burns (1759–96)

My Love is to the Light of Lights

My love is to the light of lights
As a gold fawn to the sun
And men, wha love ocht else, to her
Their ways ha' scarce begun.

3

For God their God's a jealous God
And keeps her frae their sight
He hasna had her lang eneuch
Himsel' to share his delight,

And kens gin he'd been worth his saut
He'd ha' made her first, no' last,
Since but a'e glimpse, a'e thocht, o' her
Discredits a' the Past.

(A'e glimpse, a'e thocht, and men might cease
To honour his tardy pooers;
And he's no' shair she winna prove
To be no' his – but oors!)

Yet praise the Past sin' but for it
We never might ha' seen her
– And still to oor een maun temper wi't
The glory that's been gi'en her.

My love she is the hardest thocht
That ony brain can ha'e,
And there is nocht worth ha'en in life
That doesna lead her way.

My love is to a' else that is
As meaning's meaning, or the sun
Men see ahint the sunlight whiles
Like lint-white water run.

Hugh MacDiarmid (1892–1978)

She Walks in Beauty

She walks in beauty, like the night
  Of cloudless climes and starry skies;
And all that's best of dark and bright
  Meet in her aspect and her eyes:
Thus mellowed to that tender light
  Which heaven to gaudy day denies.

One shade the more, one ray the less,
  Had half impaired the nameless grace
Which waves in every raven tress,
  Or softly lightens o'er her face;
Where thoughts serenely sweet express
  How pure, how dear their dwelling-place.

And on that cheek, and o'er that brow,
  So soft, so calm, yet eloquent,
The smiles that win, the tints that glow,
  But tell of days in goodness spent,
A mind at peace with all below,
  A heart whose love is innocent!

George Gordon, Lord Byron (1788–1824)

Shores

If we were in Talisker on the shore
where the great white foaming mouth of water
opens between two jaws as hard as flint –
the Headland of Stones and the Red Point –
I'd stand forever by the waves
renewing love out of their crumpling graves

as long as the sea would be going over
the Bay of Talisker forever;
I would stand there by the filling tide
till Preshal bowed his stallion head.

And if the two of us were together
on the shores of Calgary in Mull
between Scotland and Tiree,
between this world and eternity,
I'd stand there till time was done
counting the sands grain by grain.
And also on Uist, on Homhsta's shore,
in the face of solitude's fierce stare,
I'd remain standing, without sleep,
while sea were ebbing, drop by drop.

And if I were on Moidart's shore
with you, my novelty of desire,
I'd offer this synthesis of love,
grain and water, sand and wave.
And were we by the shelves of Staffin
where the huge joyless sea is coughing
stones and boulders from its throat,
I'd build a fortified wall
against eternity's savage howl.

Sorley Maclean (b. 1911) trans. from Gaelic (*Dain do Eimhir*) by Iain Crichton Smith

I Will Make You Brooches

I will make you brooches and toys for your delight
Of bird-song at morning and star-shine at night.
I will make a palace fit for you and me
Of green days in forests and blue days at sea.

I will make my kitchen, and you shall keep your room,
Where white flows the river and bright blows the broom,
And you shall wash your linen and keep your body white
In rainfall at morning and dewfall at night.

And this shall be for music when no one else is near,
The fine song for singing, the rare song to hear!
That only I remember, that only you admire,
Of the broad road that stretches and the roadside fire.

Robert Louis Stevenson (1850–94)

The Ship

Here is a ship you made
Out of my breasts and sides
As I lay dead in the yards
Under the hammers.

Here is a hull you built
Out of a heart of salt,
Sky-rent, the prey of birds
Strung on the longshore.

Here is her rigging bound
Nerve, sinew, ice and wind
Blowing through the night
The starred dew of beads.

Here her ribs of silver
Once steerless in a culvert
Climb the laddered centuries
To hide a cloud in a frame.

J. F. Hendry (1912–1986)

May Poem

O lusty May with Flora quene,
The balmy dropis from Phebus schene
Preluciand bemes befoir the day.
Be that Diana growis grene
Throwch glaidnes of this lusty May.

Than Esperus that is so bricht
Till wofull hairtis castis his lycht
With bankis that blumes on every bray,
And schuris ar sched furth of thair sicht
Thruch glaidnes of this lusty May.

Birdis on bewis of every birth
Rejosing nottis makand thair mirth
Rycht plesandly upoun the spray
With flurissingis our field and firth
Thruch glaidnes of this lusty May.

schene = bright	bewis = boughs
be that = by means of that	firth = wood

All luvaris that ar in cair,
To thair ladeis thay do repair
In fresch mornyngis befoir the day,
And ar in mirth ay mair and mair
Thruch glaidnes of this lusty May.

Anon. (c. 1500)

Country Girl

I make seven circles, my love
For your good breaking.
I make the gray circle of bread
And the circle of ale
And I drive the butter round in a golden ring
And I dance when you fiddle
And I turn my face with the turning sun till your
 feet come in from the field.
My lamp throws a circle of light,
Then you lie for an hour in the hot unbroken
 circle of my arms.

George Mackay Brown (b. 1921)

Watching You Walk

Watching you walk slowly across a stage,
Suddenly I am become aware of all the past;
Of all the tragic maids and queens of every age,
Of Joan, whose love the flames could not arrest.

9

Of those to whom always love was the first duty,
Who saw behind the crooked world the ugly and weak,
Whose kindliness was no gesture; no condescending pity
Could rule their actions; those whom Time broke,

But whom he could not totally destroy.
Hearing the truth you give to these dead words,
Whose writer feared the life they might enjoy,
I can recall the mating orchestra of birds

Behind your voice, as lying by the lake,
You read me Owen, and I, too deeply moved,
Watched the swans for a moment, before I spoke
The trivialities, unable to tell you how I loved.

Watching your fingers curl about a painted death,
I am suddenly glad that it is April, that you are queen
Of all the sordid marches of my bruised heart,
That, loving you, the poplars never seemed to green.

Glad of my lonely walk beside the shrunken river,
Thinking of you while seeing the tufts of ash,
The chestnut candles and unreal magnolia's wax flower;
Glad that, in loving you, the whole world lives afresh.

Ruthven Todd (1914–1978)

We Shall Never Want

Och, we shall never want, witch, you and I,
The gowd that is hairt's richest tresorie –
Come aa the hazards that on Eros tend
We hae a gowden hoard put bye
   – A million in memorie.

Dailie, weeklie, we brenn aa the bonds
And princelie squander luve til the fowr airts
Yet dailie, weeklie, it itsel renews
For ase o' spendthrift luve is Eros' gowd
  —Luve's queerest alchemie.

Tho' we want muckle and want maistlie time
— In time we're trulie beggars o' the bluid —
Yet aa o' time is ours and will be aye.
For us the naitural laws suspend:
  — Is pairt o' the tresorie.

Och, we shall never want, witch, you and I,
Tho' we be gangrels born and broken men
Our private mint's in Aphrodite's kist
And sae our credit's bundless as the main
  — Sae rich, witch, are we.

                    Sydney Goodsir Smith (1915–75)

Reasons

> Sweet one I love you
> for your lovely shape,
> for the art you make
> in paint and bed and rhyme,
> but most because we see
> into each other's hearts,
> there to read secrets
> and to trust,
> and cancel time.

                    Tom McGrath (b. 1940)

Song

Why should your face so please me
That if one little line should stray
Bewilderment would seize me
And drag me down the tortuous way
Out of the moon into the night?
But so, into this tranquil light
You raise me.

How could our minds so marry
That, separate, blunder to and fro,
Make for a point, miscarry,
And blind as headstrong horses go?
Though now they in their promised land
At pleasure travel hand in hand
Or tarry.

This concord is an answer
To questions far beyond our mind
Whose image is a dancer.
All effort is to ease refined
Here, weight is light; this is the dove
Of love and peace, not heartless love
The lancer.

Edwin Muir (1887–1959)

The Dart of Love

The dart of love as piercing flies
As the seven-grooved spear to fling;
Brown maiden of the liquid eyes,
Warm as my plaid the love I bring.

The damsel there who sang so sweet,
She in a chair of gold demure,
A silken carpet 'neath her feet,
Myself I blessed her face so pure.

Sweet are the birds beside the sea,
Sweet are the swans upon the mere,
Sweeter my lover's voice to me
When a song she pours in mine ear.

O'er the meadows on a calm day
Sweeter than mavis unto me
My lover's voice, a ho, a hey,
Beautiful maid my love is she.

Sweeter to me her kissing lip
Than the honey and the spruce-tree beer,
Though we twain the mead were to sip
From two glasses together here.

Anon., trans. from Gaelic

O Gin My Love Were Yon Red Rose

O gin my love were yon red rose,
That grows upon the castle wall,
And I myself a drap of dew
Into her bonny breast to fall;
O then, beyond expression blest,
I'd feast on beauty all the night,
Seal'd on her silk-saft falds to rest,
Till fley'd away by Phoebus' light!

Anon.

fley'd = frightened

Wooings

Love Charm

It is not love knowledge to thee
To draw water through a reed,
But the love of him (her) thou choosest,
With his warmth to draw to thee.

Arise thou early on the day of the Lord,
To the broad flat flag,
Take with thee the biretta of a priest,
And the pinnacled canopy.

Lift them on thy shoulder
In a wooden shovel,
Get thee nine stems of ferns
Cut with an axe,

The three bones of an old man,
That have been drawn from the grave,
Burn them on a fire of faggots,
And make them all into ashes.

Shake it in the very breast of thy lover,
Against the sting of the north wind,
And I will pledge, and warrant thee,
That man (woman) will never leave thee.

Anon., trans. from Gaelic

Lochinvar

O young Lochinvar is come out of the west,
Through all the wide Border his steed was the best;
And save his good broadsword he weapons had none,
He rode all unarm'd, and he rode all alone.
So faithful in love, and so dauntless in war,
There never was knight like the young Lochinvar.

He staid not for brake, and he stopp'd not for stone,
He swam the Eske river where ford there was none;
But ere he alighted at Netherby gate,
The bride had consented, the gallant came late:
For a laggard in love, and a dastard in war,
Was to wed the fair Ellen of brave Lochinvar.

So boldly he enter'd the Netherby Hall,
Among bride's-men, and kinsmen, and brothers and all:
Then spoke the bride's father, his hand on his sword,
(For the poor craven bridegroom said never a word,)
'O come ye in peace here, or come ye in war,
Or to dance at our bridal, young Lord Lochinvar?'

'I long woo'd your daughter, my suit you denied; –
Love swells like the Solway, but ebbs like its tide –
And now I am come, with this lost love of mine,
To lead but one measure, drink one cup of wine.
There are maidens in Scotland more lovely by far,
That would gladly be bride to the young Lochinvar.'

The bride kiss'd the goblet: the knight took it up,
He quaff'd off the wine, and he threw down the cup.
She look'd down to blush, and she look'd up to sigh,
With a smile on her lips and a tear in her eye.

He took her soft hand, ere her mother could bar, –
'Now tread we a measure!' said young Lochinvar.

So stately his form, and so lovely her face,
That never a hall such a galliard did grace;
While her mother did fret, and her father did fume,
And the bridegroom stood dangling his bonnet and plume;
And the bride-maidens whisper'd, 't'were better by far
To have match'd our fair cousin with young Lochinvar.'

One touch to her hand, and one word in her ear,
When they reach'd the hall-door, and the charger stood near;
So light to the croupe the fair lady he swung,
So light to the saddle before her he sprung!
'She is won! we are gone, over bank, bush, and scaur;
They'll have fleet steeds that follow', quoth young Lochinvar.

There was mounting 'mong Graemes of the Netherby clan;
Forsters, Fenwicks, and Musgraves, they rode and they ran:
There was racing and chasing on Cannobie Lee,
But the lost bride of Netherby ne'er did they see.
So daring in love, and so dauntless in war,
Have ye e'er heard of gallant like young Lochinvar?

Sir Walter Scott (1771–1832)

Shepherdess

All day my sheep have mingled with yours. They strayed
Into your valley seeking a change of ground.
Held and bemused with what they and I had found,
Pastures and wonders, heedlessly I delayed.

19

Now it is late. The tracks leading home are steep,
The stars and landmarks in your country are strange.
How can I take my sheep back over the range?
Shepherdess, show me now where I may sleep.

Norman Cameron (1905–53)

For Bonny Elspeth

I canna thole thae fleechin folk
    Wha ca' a lassie 'goddess'
When a' their meanin is to poke
    Their neb inside her bodice.
They're unco free wi' terms like 'Muse',
    'Parnassus', 'wreaths o' myrtle' –
Ay, but the mount they hae in view's
    Her ain aneath a kirtle!

Wi' sic, an they be gi'en their boon,
    The compliments they've paid ye
Are dangit aff-hand like auld shoon
    An' barefit gaes the lady.
Sic phraisin flatt'ries I abhor
    An' leave to ither gentry;
I'd sooner be tongue-dry afore,
    An', after, complimentary.

I grant fu' readily, I feel
    The influence o' your beauty –
Indeed t'wad turn a saint a de'il,
    Ev'n juvenate Auld Clootie;

20

But tho' I hae the art to please
 Wi' words as weel as onie,
I wadna at ane straik, like bees,
 Surrender a' my honey.

Syne poets, let them clink sae sweet,
 Maun jangle starv'd o' kissin,
Syne ainlie angels can complete
 Their luve wi' ane part missin,
Syne fainness follows flesh an' bluid
 By Nature's dear designin –
Lets mak the inclination guid
 By hazard o' combinin!

      Hamish Macbride (b. 1927)

O Tell Me How to Woo Thee

If doughty deeds my ladye please,
 Right soon I'll mount my steed;
And strong his arm, and fast his seat,
 That bears frae me the meed.
I'll wear thy colours in my cap,
 Thy picture in my heart;
And he that bends not to thine eye,
 Shall rue it to his smart.

 Then tell me how to woo thee, love;
  O tell me how to woo thee!
 For thy dear sake, nae care I'll take,
  Tho' ne'er another trow me.

If gay attire delight thine eye,
    I'll dight me in array;
I'll tend thy chamber door all night,
    And squire thee all the day.
If sweetest sounds can win thy ear,
    These sounds I'll strive to catch;
Thy voice I'll steal to woo thysel',
    That voice that nane can match.

But if fond love thy heart can gain,
    I never broke a vow;
Nae maiden lays her skaith to me,
    I never loved but you.
For you alone I ride the ring,
    For you I wear the blue;
For you alone I strive to sing,
    O tell me how to woo!

Robert Graham of Gartmore (c. 1735–97)

Dogs and Wolves

Across eternity, across her snows,
I see my undictated songs:
I see the traces of their paws
dappling the whiteness of the snows,
bristles in tumult, blood on their tongues.
Slender wolves and slender dogs,
leaping across walls and dykes
hurrying below barren twigs,
taking the narrow paths of glens,
seeking the sheer and windy hills.
Hear the music of their wails
on the harsh levels of our time,

22

eternal barking in my ears.
This pace is tearing at my mind.
Race of the terrible dogs and wolves
hard on the tender tracks of deer,
straight through the woods without veering,
straight to the summits without sheering,
the mild furious dogs of poetry,
wolves on the single track of beauty,
beauty of face, beauty of soul,
the white deer on plain and hill,
deer of your beauty, calm and bright,
they're hunting you by day and night.

Sorley Maclean (b. 1911) trans. from Gaelic (*Dain do Eimhir*)
by Iain Crichton Smith

Captain Wedderburn's Courtship

The Lord of Rosslyn's daughter gaed through the wud her
    lane,
And there she met Captain Wedderburn, a servant to the
    king.
He said unto his livery-man, Were't na agen the law,
I wad tak her to my ain bed, and lay her at the wa.

'I'm walking here my lane,' she says, 'amang my father's
    trees;
And ye may lat me walk my lane, kind sir, now gin ye please.
The supper-bell it will be rung, and I'll be missed awa;
Sae I'll na lie in your bed, at neither stock nor wa.'

He said, My pretty lady, I pray lend me your hand,
And ye'll hae drums and trumpets always at your command;
And fifty men to guard ye wi, that weel their swords can
   draw;
Sae we'll baith lie in ae bed, and ye'll lie at the wa.

. . . .

Then he lap aff his milk-white steed, and set the lady on,
And a' the way he walkd on foot, he held her by the hand;
He held her by the middle jimp, for fear that she should fa;
Saying, I'll tak ye to my ain bed, and lay thee at the wa.

He took her to his quartering-house, his landlady looked ben,
Saying, Monie a pretty ladie in Edinbruch I've seen;
But sic 'na pretty ladie is not into it a':
Gae, mak for her a fine down-bed, and lay her at the wa.

'O haud awa frae me, kind sir, I pray ye lat me be,
For I'll na lie in your bed till I get dishes three;
Dishes three maun be dressed for me, gif I should eat them a',
Before I lie in your bed, at either stock or wa.

''T is I maun hae to my supper a chicken without a bane;
And I maun hae to my supper a cherry without a stane;
And I maun hae to my supper a bird without a gaw,
Before I lie in your bed, at either stock or wa.'

'Whan the chicken's in the shell, I am sure it has na bane;
And whan the cherry's in the bloom, I wat is has na stane;
The dove she is a genty bird, she flees without a gaw;
Sae we'll baith lie in ae bed, and ye'll be at the wa.'

24

'O haud awa frae me, kind sir, I pray ye give me owre,
For I'll na lie in your bed, till I get presents four;
Presents four ye maun gie me, and that is twa and twa,
Before I lie in your bed, at either stock or wa.

''T is I maun hae some winter fruit that in December grew;
And I maun hae a silk mantil that waft gaed never through;
A sparrow's horn, a priest unborn, this nicht to join us twa,
Before I lie in your bed, at either stock or wa.'

'My father has some winter fruit that in December grew;
My mither has a silk mantil the waft gaed never through;
A sparrow's horn ye soon may find, there's ane on evry claw,
And twa upo the gab o it, and ye shall get them a'.

'The priest he stands without the yett, just ready to come in;
Nae man can say he eer was born, nae man without he sin;
He was haill cut frae his mither's side, and frae the same let fa;
Sae we'll baith lie in ae bed, and ye'se lie at the wa.'

'O haud awa frae me, kind sir, I pray don't me perplex,
For I'll na lie in your bed till ye answer questions six:
Questions six ye maun answer me, and that is four and twa,
Before I lie in your bed, at either stock or wa.

'O what is greener than the gress, what's higher than thae
    trees?
O what is worse than women's wish, what's deeper than the
    seas?
What bird craws first, what tree buds first, what first does on
    them fa?
Before I lie in your bed, at either stock or wa.'

'Death is greener than the gress, heaven higher than thae
    trees;
The devil's waur than women's wish, hell's deeper than the
    seas;
The cock craws first, the cedar buds first, dew first on them
    does fa;
Sae we'll baith lie in ae bed, and ye'se lie at the wa.'

Little did this lady think, that morning whan she raise,
That this was for to be the last o a' her maiden days.
But there's na into the king's realm to be found a blither twa,
And now she's Mrs. Wedderburn, and she lies at the wa.

Anon.

Tweedside

When Maggie and I were acquaint
    I carried my noddle fu' hie;
Nae lintwhite on a' the green plain,
    Nae gowdspink sae happy as me.
But I saw her sae fair, and I lo'ed,
    I wooed, but I cam' nae great speed;
So now I maun wander abroad,
    And lay my banes far frae the Tweed.

To Maggie my love I did tell,
    Saut tears did my passion express;
Alas! for I lo'ed her o'erweel,
    And the women lo'e sic a man less.

lintwhite = linnet   gowdspink = goldfinch

Her heart it was frozen and cauld,
  Her pride had my ruin decreed;
Therefore I will wander abroad,
  And lay my banes far frae the Tweed.

Lord Yester (1646–1713)

First Love

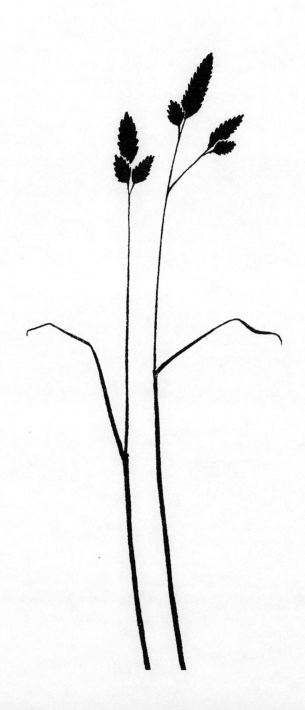

When I Roved a Young Highlander

When I roved a young Highlander o'er the dark heath,
  And climbed thy steep summit, oh Morven of snow!
To gaze on the torrent that thunder'd beneath,
  Or the mist of the tempest that gather'd below,
Untutor'd by science, a stranger to fear,
  And rude as the rocks where my infancy grew,
No feeling, save one, to my bosom was dear;
  Need I say, my sweet Mary, 'twas centred in you?

Yet it could not be love, for I knew not the name, –
  What passion can dwell in the heart of a child?
But still I perceive an emotion the same
  As I felt, when a boy, on the crag-cover'd wild:
One image alone on my bosom impress'd,
  I loved my bleak regions, not panted for new;
And few were my wants, for my wishes were bless'd:
  And pure were my thoughts, for my soul was with you.

I arose with the dawn; with my dog as my guide,
  From mountain to mountain I bounded along;
I breasted the billows of Dee's rushing tide,
  And heard at a distance the Highlander's song:
At eve, on my heath-cover'd couch of repose,
  No dreams, save of Mary, were spread to my view;
And warm to the skies my devotions arose,
  For the first of my prayers was a blessing on you.

I left my bleak home, and my visions are gone;
  The mountains are vanish'd, my youth is no more;
As the last of my race I must wither alone,
  And delight but in days I have witness'd before:
Ah! splendour has raised but embitter'd my lot;
  More dear were the schemes which my infancy knew:

31

Though my hopes may have fail'd, yet they are not forgot;
  Though cold is my heart, still it lingers with you.

When I see some dark hill point its crest to the sky,
  I think of the rocks that o'ershadow Colbleen;
When I see the soft blue of a love-speaking eye,
  I think of those eyes that endear'd the rude scene;
When, haply, some light-waving locks I behold,
  That faintly resemble my Mary's in hue,
I think on the long, flowing ringlets of gold,
  The locks that were sacred to beauty, and you.

Yet the day may arrive when the mountains once more
  Shall rise to my sight in their mantles of snow:
But while these soar above me, unchanged as before,
  Will Mary be there to receive me? – ah, no!
Adieu, then, ye hills, where my childhood was bred!
  Thou sweet flowing Dee, to thy waters adieu!
No home in the forest shall shelter my head, –
  Ah! Mary, what home could be mine but with you?

                    George Gordon, Lord Byron (1788–1824)

First Love

I have been in this garden of unripe fruit
    All the long day,
Where cold and clear from the hard green apples
    The light fell away.

I was wandering here with my own true love,
    But as I bent o'er,
She dwindled back to her childhood again
    And I saw her no more.

A wind sprang up and a hail of buds
    About me rolled,
Then this fog I knew before I was born
    But now – cold, cold!

Hugh MacDiarmid (1892–1978)

Of My First Love

O my first love! You are in my life forever
Like the EAS-COUL-AULIN* in Sutherlandshire
Where the Amhainnan Loch Bhig burn
Plunges over the desolate slopes of Leitir Dubh.
Silhouetted against grim black rocks
This foaming mountain torrent
With its source in desolate tarns
Is savage in the extreme
As its waters with one wild leap
Hurl over the dizzy brink
Of the perpendicular cliff-face
In that great den of nature,
To be churned into spray
In the steaming depths below.
Near its base the fall splits up
Into cascades spreading out like a fan.

* Name of waterfall, meaning, in Gaelic, tresses of hair.

A legend tells how a beautiful maiden
In desperation threw herself
Over the cataract – the waters
Immediately took on the shape
Of her waving hair,
And on moonlight nights she is still to be seen
Lying near the base of the fall,
Gazing up at the tremendous cascade
Of some six hundred feet!
O my first love! Even so you lie
Near the base of my precipitous, ever lonelier and colder life
With your fair hair still rippling out
As I remember it between my fingers
When you let me unloosen first
(Over thirty chaotic years ago!)
That golden tumult forever!

Hugh MacDiarmid (1892–1978)

A Memory, Now Distant

Beauty's a rose, a shining sword, a thief;
   Beauty's a singing flute, the narrow flame
That lights the incense-smoke of all belief.
   Beauty was You, and You were Beauty's name
When I was young: rose, thief, and cutting sword,
   The flute, the flame – I lost my peace to this,
Reached up for that, bled here, and there adored,
   Nor, thus bewildered, thought my state amiss.

Youth gives his heart away, for youth's ill fortune
   Is often to have nothing else to give:
Where others bargain, he must still importune –
   You laughed, and found a fuller life to live.
You were not rich because of me, it's true,
   But I was bankrupt quite because of you.

Eric Linklater (1899–1974)

Recollection of First Love

When I recall your form and face
More than you I recall
To come into a meeting-place
Where no leaves fall:
The years walk round this secret garth
But cannot change its guarded earth.

I have known women fonder far
Than you; more fair, more kind:
Women whose passionate faces are
Flowers in the mind:
But as a tall tree, stem on stem,
Your presence overshadows them.

They quicken from my sentient day
And stir my body's need;
But you had fixéd roots ere they
Down-dropped in seed:
They can but copy all I found
When you alone grew in this ground.

You are reborn from changeless loam
And are a changeless shade:
Your feet had paced the paths to Rome
Ere Rome was made:
Under your eyes great towers down fell
Before that Trojan citadel.

Time, who is knocking at the gate,
Cannot make you all his boast:
Our garden shall be desolate
But you – a ghost
Timeless; as beauty's timeless norm
You are in passion and in form.

William Soutar (1898–1943)

Youth and Love

Once only by the garden gate
  Our lips we joined and parted.
I must fulfil an empty fate
  And travel the uncharted.

Hail and farewell! I must arise,
  Leave here the fatted cattle,
And paint on foreign lands and skies
  My Odyssey of battle.

The untented Kosmos my abode,
  I pass, a wilful stranger:
My mistress still the open road
  And the bright eyes of danger.

Come ill or well, the cross, the crown,
   The rainbow or the thunder,
I fling my soul and body down
   For God to plough them under.

          Robert Louis Stevenson (1850–94)

Longing and
Waiting

Between Appointments

It has all to be experienced
in such a short time, intensively:
your habitual lateness thus disturbs
to an exaggerated degree.
It is those five minutes without you,
between half past and twenty-five to,
which I deeply, for ever, regret.
So much so that for the remaining
fifty-five I read you a lecture
on the virtues of being punctual
this time, last time, next time, every time.
Otherwise, much as I adore you,
we shall not meet again. The suspense
of waiting, always waiting, for you
makes anticipation rewarding
to such an extent that your presence
can only be an anti-climax.

Giles Gordon (b. 1940)

Christmas Letter Home
(To my sister in Aberdeen)

Drifting and innocent and sad like snow,
Now memories tease me, wherever I go,
And I think of the glitter of granite and distances
And against the blue air the lovely and bare trees,
And slippery pavements spangled with delight
Under the needles of a winter's night,
And I remember the dances, with scarf and cane,
Strolling home in the cold with the silly refrain

Of a tune by Cole Porter or Irving Berlin
Warming a naughty memory up like gin,
And Bunny and Sheila and Joyce and Rosemary
Chattering on sofas or preparing tea,
With their delicate voices and their small white hands
This is the sorrow everyone understands.
More than Rostov's artillery, more than the planes
Skirting the cyclonic islands, this remains,
The little, lovely taste of youth we had:
The guns and not our silliness were mad,
All the unloved and ugly seeking power
Were mad, and not our trivial evening hour
Of swirling taffetas and muslin girls,
Oh, not their hands, their profiles, or their curls,
Oh, not the evenings of coffee and sherry and snow,
Oh, not the music. Let us rise and go –
But then the months and oceans lie between,
And once again the dust of spring, the green
Bright beaks of buds upon the poplar trees,
And summer's strawberries, and autumn's ease,
And all the marble gestures of the dead,
Before my eyes caress again your head,
Your tiny strawberry mouth, your bell of hair,
Your blue eyes with their deep and shallow stare,
Before your hand upon my arm can still
The nerves that everything but home makes ill:
In this historic poster-world I move,
Noise, movement, emptiness, but never love.
Yet all this grief we had to have my dear,
And most who grieve have never known, I fear,
The lucky streak for which we die and live,
And to the luckless must the lucky give
All trust, all energy, whatever lies
Under the anger of democracies:
Whatever strikes the towering torturer down,

42

Whatever can outface the bully's frown,
Talk to the stammerer, spare a cigarette
For tramps at midnight ... oh, defend it yet!
Some Christmas I shall meet you. Oh, and then
Though all the boys you used to like are men,
Though all my girls are married, though my verse
Has pretty steadily been growing worse,
We shall be happy: we shall smile and say,
'These years! It only seems like yesterday
I saw you sitting in that very chair.'
'You have not changed the way you do your hair.'
'These years were painful, then?' 'I hardly know.
Something lies gently over them, like snow,
A sort of numbing white forgetfulness ...'

And so, good night, this Christmas, and God bless!

G. S. Fraser (1914–1980)

Fiddler's Song

The storm is over, lady.
The sea makes no more sound.
What do you wait for, lady?
His yellow hair is drowned.

The waves go quiet, lady,
Like sheep into the fold.
What do you wait for, lady?
His kissing mouth is cold.

George Mackay Brown (b. 1921)

43

Arrivals 1

The plane meets
Its reflection on the wet
Runway, then crosses
To where I wait
Behind plate glass.

I watch
With a mixture of longing and despair
As you re-enter
The real world.

All we have is each other.
I sometimes wonder
If that is enough;
Whether being together
Enlarges or diminishes grief.

Stewart Conn (b. 1936)

Near Midnight

I hear a bull blaring
From the sad shores of love.

Owls never haunt
The dark rides of this darkness,
So the one now calling over
The hayfield has the voice
Of a prophet returned
From the wilderness.

What wilderness shall I
Go into so that you will listen
When I return?

Under the few stars
Terns are dipping through the air
Towards the green islet
They rest on, quarrel on.
Though they seem half
Reptile, half angel, they
Are closer to me
Than you.
Their silence frightens me
Less than yours. – I listen,
I listen, and hear only
Reeds whispering their language and
A bull – sailor on shore
Calling the sirens in.
And all this
Is wilderness enough
For me.

Norman MacCaig (b. 1910)

Anemones

Anemones, they say, are out
  By sheltered woodland streams,
With budding branches all about
  Where Spring-time sunshine gleams;

Such are the haunts they love, but I
    With swift remembrance see
Anemones beneath a sky
    Of cold austerity –

Pale flowers too faint for winds so chill
    And with too fair a name –
That day I lingered on a hill
    For one who never came.

                    Marion Angus (1866–1946)

The Trout of the Well

Thou speckled little trout so fair,
The lover of my love, o where?
Is he beyond the ocean's storm,
With heroes holding combat warm?

Thou speckled little trout so fair,
The lover of my mind, o where?
Out on the gloom-hills doth he stride,
Cairn-brownie maiden at his side?

Thou speckled little trout so fair,
The lover of my heart, o where?
The Isle of Youth, is that his bound,
The champions of old around?

Thou speckled little trout so fair,
The lover of my breast, o where?
In Ireland or in Alba steep?
Behind the sun is he asleep?

Thou speckled little trout so fair,
Is with my love MacMary there?
And may I let my sorrow go
In the unfailing River's flow?

Thou speckled little trout so fair,
My lover, o my lover where?

Anon., trans. from Gaelic

Reproaches

They are pulling down that London hotel
where I slept alone in a double bed
rather than deny my half of the dream.

A new Labour Exchange has been opened
to accommodate those people I put off
to see you, on days when you could not come.

The swans no longer bother to patrol
the lake in the park, and those small flowers
you were fond of have been taken away.

After the Haydn symphony, the man
with the baton announced there was no point
in playing Mahler to your empty seat.

47

Now the post office has decided to suspend
deliveries, and they can blow up
the rest of the world too, for all I care.

W. Price Turner (b. 1927)

A Letter

Tonight I'll meet you: yes, tonight. I know
There are, perhaps, a thousand miles – but not
Tonight. Tonight I go inside. I take
All the walls down, the bric-a-brac, the trash,
The tawdry pungent dust these months have gathered
Into a heap about me. I must prepare
And somehow move away from the slow world,
The circling menace with its throat and teeth
Attempting definition; and brush off
Those thoughts that, clinging like thin fallen hairs,
Make me unclean; for I must go tonight
And, secret from my shadow, go alone
Back to the hour when you yourself became
So much my own that even my own eyes
Seemed strange compared to you who were a new
Complete pervasive organ of all sense
Through which I saw and heard and more than touched
The very dignity of experience.

Burns Singer (1928–64)

from Sang on Absence

The faithful messinger, which is the nicht
To luifars langerous,
Augments my woe, and als the dayis licht
Maks me more dolorous.
The day I dwyne,
The nicht I pyne;
Evin eikis my sorow
Wors then the morow.
O God, in love if be malhourous.

And if that neid to slumber me constraine,
Faint throuch melancolie,
Unrest dois quickly walkin me again
To muse miseris.
Whatevir chance
Dois me outrance
Saif fals thinking
In sueit dreming. O dreame maist sueit, if it war not a lie!

In cairful bed full oft, in myne intent,
To twitche I do appear,
Now syde, now breist, now sueit mow redolent
Of that sueit bodye deir.
I stretch my hand
In vain ernand;
My luif is far,
And not found nar,
O scorne of luifars, Cupid blind art heir!

Attrib. to King James I of Scotland (1394–1437)

dwyne = dwindle   outrance = extremity

49

O Western Wind

O western wind, when wilt thou blow
That the small wind down can rain?
Christ, if my love were in my arms,
And I in my bed again.

                              Anon.

Encounters

Maggie Lauder

Wha wad na be in love
  Wi' bonny Maggie Lauder?
A piper met her gaun to Fife,
  And speir'd what was't they ca'd her;
Right scornfully she answer'd him,
  Begone you hallanshaker,
Jog on your gate, you bladderskate,
  My name is Maggie Lauder.

Maggie, quoth he, and by my bags
  I'm fidgin fain to see thee;
Sit down by me, my bonny bird,
  In troth I winna steer thee;
For I'm a piper to my trade,
  My name is Rob the Ranter,
The lasses loup as they were daft,
  When I blaw up my chanter.

Piper, quoth Meg, hae you your bags,
  Or is your drone in order?
If you be Rob, I've heard of you;
  Live you upo' the Border?
The lasses a', baith far and near,
  Have heard of Rob the Ranter;
I'll shake my foot wi' right goodwill,
  If you'll blaw up your chanter.

Then to his bags he flew wi' speed,
  About the drone he twisted;
Meg up and wallop'd o'er the green,
  For brawly could she frisk it.
Weel done, quoth he, play up, quoth she,
  Weel bob'd, quoth Rob the Ranter,

'Tis worth my while to play indeed,
    When I hae sic a dancer.

Weel hae you play'd your part, quoth Meg,
    Your cheeks are like the crimson,
There's nane in Scotland plays sae weel,
    Since we lost Habbie Simson.
I've liv'd in Fife, baith maid and wife,
    These ten years and a quarter;
Gin you should come to Enster fair,
Speir you for Maggie Lauder.

Attrib. to Francis Sempill of Beltrees
(?1616–?1685)

Comin' Thro' the Rye

Comin' thro' the rye, poor body,
    Comin' thro' the rye;
She draigl't a' her petticoatie,
    Comin' thro' the rye.

Oh, Jenny's a' weet, poor body,
    Jenny's seldom dry;
She draigl't a' her petticoatie,
    Comin' thro' the rye.

Gin a body meet a body
    Comin' thro 'the rye;
Gin a body kiss a body,
    Need a body cry?

Gin a body meet a body
   Comin' thro' the glen,
Gin a body kiss a body,
   Need the warld ken?

Robert Burns (1759–96)

The White Stallion

There was that horse
   that I found then
   my white one
big tall and lean as
   and mean as hell.

And people who saw me
   would stare as I passed them
   and say
     'Look at him ...
   how he rides his cock-horse.'

But my steed
   the white stallion
stormed into the moonlight
   and on it was me.

There were those girls
   that I found then
   my loved ones
small fat and lean ones
   and virgins as well.

And those girls who saw me
would weep as I passed them
and cry
'Look at him ...
how he rides his cock-horse.'

But my steed
the white stallion
went proud in the still night
and on it was me.

There was one girl
that I loved then –
a woman –
as tall and as lithe as
a woman should be.

And soon as I saw her
I dismounted my stallion
to stay
by the woman
whose love I required.

But my steed
the white stallion
rode off in the moonlight
and on it was she.

Goodbye to the horse
to the woman
and stallion.
Farewell to my cock-horse
and loving as well.

To people who see me
    and stare as I pass them
    I wail
        'Look at me ...
    I once rode a cock-horse.'

But my steed
    the white stallion
is lost in the moonlight
    and on it rides she.

Pete Morgan (b. 1939)

The Tryst

O luely, luely, cam she in
And luely she lay doun:
I kent her be her caller lips
And her breists sae sma' and roun'.

A' thru the nicht we spak nae word
Nor sinder'd bane frae bane:
A' thru the nicht I heard her hert
Gang soundin' wi' my ain.

It was about the waukrife hour
When cocks begin to craw
That she smool'd saftly thru the mirk
Afore the day wud daw.

57

Sae luely, luely, cam she in
Sae luely was she gaen;
And wi' her a' my simmer days
Like they had never been.

William Soutar (1898–1943)

At First Sight

Should I speak unthinkingly,
rashly, outwardly,
or look, wordlessly?

Move determinedly
or wait expectantly?
She sighs slightly.

I turn anxiously.
She sits quietly,
smiling distantly.

Either lie, passionately,
or not lie, fruitlessly?
I pause, two-mindedly.

To love wishfully,
blindly, entirely,
self-transformingly;

or to stay truthfully
in doubt, wistfully
doomed to reality?

Her face, held beautifully,
looks at me questioningly.
I watch her, wonderingly.

To love recklessly,
hazarding certainty,
losing identity;

or to feel warily –
vows made conditionally,
words weighed carefully?

She looks up suddenly,
her eyes speaking clearly
my thought, completely.

Poised unbelievably,
we touch magically,
and light strikes, blindingly.

                              Alastair Reid (b. 1926)

Birth of a Genius Among Men

The night folded itself about me like a woman's hair.
Thousands of dispersed forces drawn as by a magnet
Streamed through the open windows – millions of stars
  poured through;
What destiny were they seeking in us, what outlet?

An immense vigour awoke in my body.
My breast expanded and overflowed into the night.
I was one with Scotland out there and with all the world
And thoughts of your beauty shone in me like starlight.

You were all female, ripe as a rose for the plucking,
I was all male and no longer resisted my need.
The earth obeyed the rhythm of our panting.
The mountains sighed with us. Infinity was emptied.

To both of us it seemed as if we had never loved before.
A miracle was abroad and I knew that not merely I
Had accomplished the act of love but the whole universe
    through me,
A great design was fulfilled, another genius nigh.

Yet I lay awake and as the daylight broke
I heard the faint voices of the Ideas discuss
The way in which they could only express themselves yet
In fragmentary and fallacious forms through us.

Hugh MacDiarmid (1892–1978)

In Glasgow

In my smoochy corner
take me on a cloud
I'll wrap you round
and lay you down
in smoky tinfoil
rings and records
sheets of whisky

and the moon all right
old pal all right
the moon all night

Mercy for the rainy
tyres and the violet
thunder that bring you
shambling and shy
from chains of Easterhouse
plains of lights
make your delight
in my nest my spell
my arms and my shell
my barn my bell

I've combed your hair
and washed your feet
and made you turn
like a dark eel
in my white bed
till morning lights
a silent cigarette
throw on your shirt
I lie staring yet
forget forget

Edwin Morgan (b. 1920)

Black Tomintoul

To Scotland came the tall American
And went to stay on a little farm
Oh it was a Scotch farm set in the wild
A wee Scotch burn and a stoney field

61

She came to a corner, it was raining
And the little trees were all leaning in
This was Scotland the way she had thought of it
Care, not gravity, makes them lean
The rain falling Scotchly, Scotchly
And the hills that did not soar up but in

But most she looked at the bull so wild
She looked at the bull with the eyes of a child
Never in New York did she see such a bull
As this great Scotch one, Tomintoul
She called him secretly, the great Scotch bull

He was black all over, even for a bull
And oh he had such a lovely hide
She saw him follow one cow aside
Tell me, please, is that cow his bride?
No, they are all his lawful br—r—ride
There were twenty-four cows on the Scotch hillside

It was almost too much for the tall American girl
She watched him stand on his opposite hill
Black Tomintoul, and he always bellowed
But afterwards something in her was mellowed.

Ian Hamilton Finlay (b. 1925)

In More's Hotel
(for Aileen)

Wasn't it just that
We touched for the first time
The mother string
The pearls are threaded on?

Or was it especially
A key, a Bible –
A litany of chance
Which found again
Would spell us close
As we were then
In More's hotel,
Learning our alphabet.

Last night it was cloud
Against the pane, twice
You dreamt it.
This morning I turn on a tap and water
Is water alone, relating
To keys and Bibles
By a cordial difference,
Not very likely, but all the same
Married and holding together well.

Robert Nye (b. 1939)

Duo

I

Bathed in her breath I basked beside her, weak
and trembling. She had burst beneath me like
A bomb, her body banging upward, teak-
Hard and beautiful, firm as a spike,
Bold as a bitch ... and a bitch she was,
Snarling once and tearing more than once;
A beast with blood upon her raking claws.

Below me, slipping from me, not an ounce
Of strength within me, a sudden spasm bent
Her backwards, arched like a bridge. A shudder, a shriek,
Collapse, and, for a moment, death. Spent,
My heart insane, without the power to speak,
I could only lie and listen to her breathing:
I could only lie and listen to her breathing.

2

Back to back until the last button tied
Us once again to our anonymity,
Clipped and casual in attempts to hide
The awkwardness of our sterility
In the aftermath's uneasy air, we made
What reparations necessary. Rain
Was pounding on the street outside. My frayed
Hair combed, my collar neat, I tried to train
My tongue to a convincing lie. 'I'll come
Again,' I said. She didn't show delight
Exactly, but smiled. 'Why not! I'm always home
About this time.' She knew the signs all right.
We kissed to the sound of my shuffling feet.
Two minutes later, I was on the street.

William Keys (b. 1928)

Romantics

from The Kingis Quair

Stanzas 41–45

And therewith kest I doun myn eye ageyne,
  Whare as I sawe, walking under the tour,
Full secretly new cummyn hir to pleyne,
  The fairest or the freschest yong floure
  That ever I sawe, me thoght, before that houre,
For which sodayn abate, anon astert
The blude of all my body to my hert.

And though I stude abaisit tho a lyte
  No wonder was, forwhy my wittis all
Were so overcom with plesance and delyte,
  Onely throu latting of myn eyen fall,
  That sudaynly my hert become hir thrall
For ever of free wyll; for of manace
There was no takyn in hir suete face.

And in my hede I drewe ryght hastily,
  And eftsones I lent it forth ageyne,
And sawe hir walk, that verray womanly,
  With no wight mo bot only women tweyne.
  Than gan I studye in myself and seyne,
'A! swete, ar ye a warldly creature,
Or hevinly thing in likeness of nature?

Or ar ye god Cupidis owin princesse,
  And cummyn ar to lous me out of band?

abate = discomfiture	wight = creature
astert = started back	gan = did
takyn = token	seyne = say

67

Or ar ye verray Nature the goddess,
　　That have depaynted with your hevinly hand
　　This gardyn full of flouris, as they stand?
What sall I think, allace! what reverence
Sall I minster to your excellence?

If ye a goddess be, and that ye like
　　To do me payne, I may it noght astert;
If ye be warldly wight, that dooth me sike,
　　Why lest God mak you so, my derrest hert,
　　To do a sely prisoner thus smert,
That lufis you all, and wote of noght bot wo?
And therefore, merci, swete! sen it is so.'

　　　　　　　King James I of Scotland (1394–1437)

astert = escape　　　　sely = wretched
that dooth me sike = who causes me to sigh

It is Na, Jean, thy Bonie Face

It is na, Jean, thy bonie face
　　Nor shape that I admire;
Altho' thy beauty and thy grace,
　　Might weel awauk desire:
Something, in ilka part o' thee,
　　To praise, to love, I find;
But dear as is thy form to me,
　　Still dearer is thy mind.

Nae mair ungen'rous wish I hae,
  Nor stronger in my breast,
Than, if I canna mak thee sae,
  At least to see thee blest.
Content am I, if Heaven shall give
  But happiness to thee:
And as wi' thee I'd wish to live,
  For thee I'd bear to die.

Robert Burns (1759–96)

Floating off to Timor

If only we'd been strangers
we'd be floating off to Timor,
we'd be shimmering on the Trades
in a blue jersey boat
with shandies, flying-fish,
a pace of dolphins
to the copra ports.
And it's no use crying
to me, What Dolphins?
for I know where they are
and I'd have snapped you up
and carried you away
if we had been strangers.

But here we are care
of the black roofs.
It's not hard to find
with a collar turned up
and a hoot from the Clyde.

The steps come home
whistling too. And a kettle
steams the cranes out slowly.
It's living with ships
makes a rough springtime
and who is safe
when they sing and blow
their music – they seem
to swing at some light rope
like those desires
we keep for strangers.
God, the yellow deck
breathes, it heaves spray
back like a shout.
We're cutting through
some straits of the world
in our old dark room
with salty wings
in the shriek of the dock wind.
But we're caught – meshed
in the fish-scales, ferries,
mudflats, lifebelts
fading into football cries
and the lamps coming on
to bring us in.

We take in
the dream, a cloth from the line
the trains fling sparks on
in our city. We're better awake.
But you know I'd take
you all the same,
if you were my next stranger.

Edwin Morgan (b. 1920)

To His Maistres

So swete a kis yistrene fra thee I reft,
In bowing down thy body on the bed,
That evin my lyfe within thy lippis I left;
Sensyne from thee my spirits wald never shed;
To folow thee it from my body fled,
And left my corps als cold as ony kie.
Bot when the danger of my death I dred,
To seik my spreit I sent my harte to thee;
Bot it wes so inamored with thyn ee,
With thee it myndit lykwyse to remane:
So thou hes keepit captive all the thrie,
More glaid to byde then to returne agane.
Except thy breath thare places had suppleit,
Even in thyn armes, thair doutles had I deit.

Alexander Montgomerie (?1545–?1610)

kie = key

With an Antique Crystal Cup and Ring

'Drinc hael!'

Noble lady, in whose light
The rosy laughing wine grows bright,
From my poor hand, O deign to take
The cup I empty for thy sake;
And when the circling year comes round,
And Christmas snows have wrapt the ground,

And in thy bright and magic bower
The lonely heart for one short hour,
Like linnets in the winter sun,
Forgets its grief as I have done –
Take the cup, and drink the wine,
'Drinc hael!' – as I to thee and thine;
And when none other thinks on me –
Say in thy heart – 'May God bless thee' –
At natal, and at bridal hour,
Drink to the blossoms of thy bower;
And every pledge of blessing said,
Heaven make it double on their head;
And O! when from life's transient cup
Thy lips have drunk their nectar up,
And left it empty, frail as this,
May the last golden drops be bliss,
And like this gem beneath the wine,
The glorious deathless jewel thine.

John Sobieski Stuart (1795–1872)

To Anybody At All

I didn't want you cosy and neat and limited.
I didn't want you to be understandable,
Understood.
I wanted you to stay mad and limitless,
Neither bound to me nor bound to anyone else's or
    your own preconceived idea of yourself.

Margaret Tait (b. 1918)

There is a Tide

There is a tide in luve's affair
Nae poem e'er was made –
The hairt hings like a gull in air
For aa the words are said.

Nou in this saagin-tide we swey
While the world wags and empires faa:
But we that burned high Ilium
What can we rack that ken it aa?

Sydney Goodsir Smith (1915–75)

At Kilbryde Castle

Through the white winter palace
of the royal forest
our horses pace on muffled hooves,
past tree-stumps upholstered with snow
like the toppled foot-stools of courtesans
who have fled the revolution,
leaving the sable stole
trailing over the rhododendrons'
ramshackle sofa.

Jilted hinds stare
into the cracked mirrors of pools
and eyes like forgotten cigarettes
in white saucers glare
as I unsheath my shotgun,
snap in two cartridges.

73

My love, you reel
in the saddle
as the black tracer
of the woodcock
bursts from the shrubbery,
and the cold war ends.

Lorn M. Macintyre (b. 1941)

The Straits

If I stare at you,
driving slate seas,
it is because I want to draw from you
all your loveliness into my own face.

I gave away the rare colours
I got from the sea-anemone,
and the stippled sheen
from a mackerel stiffening.

Strength was a beauty I thieved
out of the line of the moorland;
  – regard its breaking
over the prominences of his skull
like the watershed of the high ridge.

His eyes,
spaced well apart,
have no pupils,
are broken windmills
slipping a hold
on the cliffs of air,

missing,
missing in rhythm.

The god had shins
like a cutting edge,
and I reached for them
never thinking
to be left with no hands.

The place is
solitary,
lain on my back on the night shore,
knobbed spine fits the pebble crevices.

From across the straits
a little rain comes
to lay the dust.

                              Valerie Gillies (b. 1948)

Young Girl

The young heroes, the generous young men,
Wasting themselves like pennies at a wedding,
Will, when the sleep of exhaustion eludes them,
Think of her face.

                         Menzies McKillop (b. 1929)

Plain as the Glistering Planets Shine

Plain as the glistering planets shine
   When winds have cleaned the skies,
Her love appeared, appealed for mine,
   And wantoned in her eyes.

Clear as the shining tapers burned
   On Cytherea's shrine,
Those brimming, lustrous beauties turned,
   And called and conquered mine.

The beacon-lamp that Hero lit
   No fairer shone on sea,
No plainlier summoned will and wit,
   Than hers encouraged me.

I thrilled to feel her influence near,
   I struck my flag at sight.
Her starry silence smote my ear
   Like sudden drums at night.

I ran as, at the cannon's roar,
   The troops the ramparts man –
As in the holy house of yore
   The willing Eli ran.

Here, lady, lo! that servant stands
   you picked from passing men,
And should you need nor heart nor hands
   He bows and goes again.

Robert Louis Stevenson (1850–94)

Personal Column

In daydream fantasies of self-indulgence
my favourite theme is the scene where
I walk into a room loaded with innocence
to be the victim of an orgy there.

The background varies, but my home will do,
where I am greeted by five lady guests,
or a strange hotel, a midnight interview:
and I gasp helpless under dabbling breasts.

Why do I stage intrigues of such dimension,
always eager to be outnumbered in the deed?
For the carnal fact is, I hasten to mention,
that I would never deny a lady in need.

When Ladies' Circles invite me to remote spots,
I accept with alacrity and warm suspicion.
I leave my door unlocked and cook in my thoughts,
but not one nymphomaniac seeks admission.

So damn all those lousy novelists who instil
sex as a fillip, larkin' around like fizz,
which makes one hanker for the pay-off thrill:
a little taste of how Orpheus got his.

W. Price Turner (b. 1927)

To My Mountain

Since I must love your north
of darkness, cold, and pain,
the snow, the lovely glen,
let me love true worth,

the strength of the hard rock,
the deafening stream of wind
that carries sense away
swifter than flowing blood.

Heather is harsh to tears
and the rough moors
give the buried face no peace
but make me rise,

and oh, the sweet scent, and purple skies!

Kathleen Raine (b. 1908)

Unromantics

A Song for an Able Bastard

I wish I loved an honest girl,
Unseeking and unsought,
Whose lips were soft as they were shy,
And not as they'd been taught.

I wish — but what's the use of that?
The only She in town
Is not so honest as she's fair —
She's light as thistle-down!

And that's my luck, for I was born
When a March moon was mad;
I wish I loved an honest girl —
I wish my father had.

Eric Linklater (1899–1974)

Marry the Lass?
(from The Irascible Poet)

Body black in the rock spine of Quinag
the thought intrudes: marry the lass?

Easy to spend a lifetime
with the minimum of fuss and sunny days ...

He dismisses the thought, and the day
is spent struggling with unyielding rock.

Through evening the return is made,
fingers loose, grey eyes on the far Atlantic —

Also recalling her mother's ballooning outlines.
Home again. The piratical poet

Decides they will instead enjoy the
fashionable fruit of living in sin,

And muttering defiantly 'Many good years yet',
takes his boots off, has a dram, forgets the matter.

Andrew Greig (b. 1951)

Nora's Vow

Here what Highland Nora said, –
'The Earlie's son I will not wed,
Should all the race of nature die,
And none be left but he and I.
For all the gold, for all the gear,
And all the lands both far and near
That ever valour lost or won,
I would not wed the Earlie's son.'

'A Maiden's vows,' old Callum spoke,
'Are lightly made and lightly broke;
The heather on the mountain's height
Begins to bloom in purple light;
The frost-wind soon shall sweep away
That lustre deep from glen and brae;
Yet Nora, ere its bloom be gone,
May blithely wed the Earlie's son.'

'The swan,' she said, 'the lake's clear breast
May barter for the eagle's nest;

The Awe's fierce stream may backward turn,
Ben-Cruaichan fall, and crush Kilchurn;
Our kilted clans, when blood is high,
Before their foes may turn and fly;
But I, were all these marvels done,
Would never wed the Earlie's son.'

Still in the water-lily's shade
Her wonted nest the wild-swan made;
Ben-Cruaichan stands as fast as ever,
Still downward foams the Awe's fierce river;
To shun the clash of foeman's steel
No Highland brogue has turn'd the heel;
But Nora's heart is lost and won,
– She's wedded to the Earlie's son!

Sir Walter Scott (1771–1832)

Love in Edinburgh

The neaps are ow'er champit
in prim Auld Reekie.
Ay, they say they get merrit for love
How mony does yon? Gey few.
Maist get merrit o'er cockie leekie –
Whisht man! where's yer Calvin noo?

Nicholas Fairbairn (b. 1933)

Lady Isabel and the Elf-Knight

My plaid awa', my plaid awa',
And o'er the hill and far awa';
And far awa' to Norrowa',
My plaid shall not be blown awa'!

Lady Isabel sits in her bower sewing,
   Aye as the gowans grow gay –
She heard an elf-knight his horn blawing,
   The first morning in May.

The elfin-knight sits on yon hill,
He blaws his horn baith loud and shrill.

He blaws it east, he blaws it west,
He blaws it where he lyketh best.

'I wish that horn were in my kist,
Yea, and the knight in my arms niest.'

She had no sooner these words said,
When that knight came to her bed.

'Thou art owre young a maid,' quoth he,
'Married with me thou ill wouldst be,'

'I have a sister younger than I,
And she was married yesterday.'

'Married with me if thou wouldst be,
A courtesie thou must do to me.

'For thou must shape a sark to me
Without any cut or hem,' quoth he.

'It's ye maun shape it knife-and-shurlesse,
And also sew it needle-threedlesse.

'And ye maun wash it in yonder well,
Where the dew never wat nor the rain never fell.

'And ye maun dry it upon a thorn
That never budded sin Adam was born.'

'Now sin ye have asked some things o' me,
It's right I ask as mony o' thee.

'My father he ask'd me an acre o' land
Between the saut sea and the strand.

'And ye maun are it wi' your blawin' horn,
And ye maun sow it wi' pepper corn.

'An ye maun harrow it with ae tyne,
And ye maun shear it with ae horse bane.

'And ye maun stack it in yon mouse-hole,
And ye maun thresh it in yon shoe-sole.

'And ye maun winnow it in your loof,
And ye maun sack it in your glove.

'And ye maun bring it owre the sea,
Fair and clean and dry to me.

'And when ye've done an' finish'd your wark
Come to me, love, an' get your sark.'

are = plough   loof = palm

85

'It's I'll not quit my plaid for my life;
It haps my seven bairns and my wife.'

The wind sall not blaw my plaid awa':
'And it's I will keep me a maiden still,
Let the elfin knight do what he will' –
The wind has not blawn my plaid awa'!

Anon.

Hey for a Lass wi' a Tocher

Awa' wi' your witchcraft o' beauty's alarms,
The slender bit beauty ye grasp in your arms:
O, gie me the lass that has acres o' charms,
O, gie me the lass wi' the weel-stockit farms.

Then hey, for a lass wi' a tocher,
Then hey, for a lass wi' a tocher;
Then hey, for a lass wi' a tocher –
The nice yellow guineas for me.

I grant ye, your Dearie is bonie and braw,
She's genty, and strappin, and stately witha';
But see yon strappin oaks at the head o' the shaw,
Wi' the whack! of an ax how stately they'll fa'.

Your beauty's a flower, in the morning that blows,
And withers the faster, the faster it grows;
But the rapturous charm o' the bonie green knowes,
Ilk Spring they're new deckit wi' bonie white yowes.

And e'en when this Beauty your bosom has blest,
The brightest o' beauty may cloy, when possest;
But the sweet yellow darlings wi' Geordie imprest,
The langer ye hae them, the mair they're carest.

Robert Burns (1759–96)

Marriages

Love

She stood in her snood and arasaid
  Beneath the trees of the wood,
The buckled plaid round her shoulder laid,
  She looked for him as she stood.

He came to her running o'er the heath,
  A present was in his hand,
And upon his dirk drawn from the sheath
  They plighted their troth to stand.

The mavis was singing in the tree,
  The lark was high in the air,
Happy was he and happy was she
  As they stood together there.

He held her close in his arms' embrace,
  Their eyes and their lips did meet,
He looked down into her lovely face,
  And her heart did faster beat.

The clouds flew over the mountain crest,
  The spray was flecking the sea,
She drew him close to her throbbing breast,
  Her prisoner for aye to be.

They went to kirk an it came the day,
  And the book the priest did take;
He in his kilt was so bright and gay
  As his promise he did make.

She stood at his side so white and fair,
  Her white fingers fair to give,

The priest handfasted them then and there,
  And he blessed them long to live.

O God give the joy and God the love
  To those who are lovers true,
Shed down benediction from above
  As in one are joined the two.

Anon., trans. from Gaelic

Love Song

Soft as the wind your hair,
gull-gleaming your breasts.
I hoard no treasures there.
I do not grope for rest.
I seek you as my home,
that all your sensitive life
may fuse into my own,
and the world match with my wife.

I carry you out of this
to no enchanted isle.
Blood is tart in your kiss,
and no dream in your smile.
Bitter, bitter the hours
and coasts of our patrol.
Foggy this Minch of ours.
But I sail with your soul.

I come to you in the flame
of a burst and broken land.
There is acid in my brain

and withering in my hand.
Your touch will plot us wise,
your quiet keep it true;
and joy be the starlight
to what we have to do.

Joseph Macleod (1902–1984)

Travelling to My Second Marriage
on the Day of the First Moonshot

We got into the carriage. It was hot.
An old woman sat there, her white hair
Stained at the temples as if by smoke.
Beside her the old man, her husband,
Talking of rivers, salmon, yearling trout,
Their dwindled waters.

A windscreen wiper on another engine
Flickered like an irritable, a mad eyelid.
The woman's mouth fell open. She complained.
Her husband said; 'I'd like
A one-way ticket to the moon.
Wouldn't mind that.'

'What for?' 'Plant roses.' '*Roses?*' 'Roses,
Yes. I'd be the first rosegrower on the moon.
Mozart, I'd call my rose. That's it.
A name for a new rose; Mozart.
That's what I'd call the first rose on the moon,
If I got there to grow it.'

93

Ten nine eight seven six five four three two one.
The old woman, remember her, and the old man:
Her black shoes tapping; his gold watch as he counted.
They'd been to a funeral. We were going to a wedding.
When the train started the wheels sang *Figaro*
And there was a smell of roses.

Robert Nye (b. 1939)

Bridal Day

This bridal day with gold I will enchain,
And wear its hours like rubies on my heart,
That you and I from Love may never part
While still these jewelled monuments remain.
These monuments, wrought out of hours, contain
The wound inflicted on me by Love's dart,
That stung with such intolerable smart,
Until to-day we vanquished Time and Pain.

And now I wear this crimson diadem
Where late my heart I did incarnadine
With open wounds in passionate array,
Unhealed until your eyes looked down at them,
And crystallized their sanguine drops to shine
In captured moments of our bridal day.

Compton Mackenzie (1883–1972)

Wedding

With a great working of elbows
The fiddlers ranted
   — *Joy to Ingrid and Magnus!*

With much boasting and burning
The whisky circled
   — *Wealth to Ingrid and Magnus!*

With deep clearings of the throat
The minister intoned
   — *Thirdly, Ingrid and Magnus.*

Ingrid and Magnus stared together
When midnight struck
At a white unbroken bed.

George Mackay Brown (b. 1921)

The Generous Gentleman

As I came in by Tiviot side,
   And by the braes of Branksome,
There first I saw my bonny bride,
   Young, smiling, sweet, and handsome:
Her skin was safter than the down,
   And white as alabaster;
Her hair a shining wavy brown;
   In straightness nane surpast her.

Life glow'd upon her lip and cheek,
   Her clear een were surprising,

And beautifully turn'd her neck,
Her little breasts just rising:
Nae silken hose with gushets fine,
Or shoon with glancing laces,
On her fair leg forbad to shine,
Well shapen native graces.

Ae little coat, and bodice white,
Was sum of a' her claithing; –
Even these o'er mickle; – mair delyte
She'd given cled wi' naithing.
She lean'd upon a flow'ry brae,
By which a burnie trotted;
On her I glowr'd my saul away,
While on her sweets I doated.

A thousand beauties of desert
Before had scarce alarm'd me,
Till this dear artless struck my heart,
And but designing, charm'd me.
Hurry'd by love, close to my breast
I grasp'd this fund of blisses;
Wha smil'd, and said, without a priest,
Sir, hope for nought but kisses.

I had nae heart to do her harm,
And yet I couldna want her;
What she demanded, ilka charm
Of her's pled, I should grant her.
Since heaven had dealt to me a routh,
Straight to the kirk I led her,
There plighted her my faith and troth,
And a young lady made her.

Allan Ramsay (1684/5–1758)

The Birthday

When we are at last in that far heaven
Where there is no more taking and giving
In marriage,
And we are pure beyond all error
Freed of delights, of joy or terror,
Without dear hands and feet,
And all that lies between, refined
Out of all knowledge –
That will be a late limbo.

But at the Day
The great mystery will open clear
And our bodies resurrect appear
Whole and without blemish;
The Fire that transmogrified the mind
Will make us again what we
Always were, before mortality.
Then may we face eternity, with equanimity.

Beforehand, in those long spaces of God's art,
I can see our earthly shapes, our bones inert
Carved perpetually with desire, and linked
In loving and anguished image
Of the unending joy to come –
The unspoken word, the patient poise
Makes a past world of deepest sense,
A life, a time, that now is making,
Let us create with honest loving.

                    Morley Jamieson (b. 1917)

From the Night-Window

The night rattles with nightmares.
Children cry in the close-packed houses,
A man rots in his snoring.
On quiet feet, policemen test doors.
Footsteps become people under streetlamps.
Drunks return from parties,
Sounding of empty bottles and old songs.
The young women come home,
The pleasure in them deafens me.
They trot like small horses
And disappear into white beds
At the edge of the night.
All windows open, this hot night.
And the sleepless, smoking in the dark,
Making small red lights at their mouths,
Count the years of their marriages.

Douglas Dunn (b. 1942)

Happy Marriage

Thou genius of connubial love, attend!
Let silent wonder all thy powers suspend,
Whilst to thy glory I devote my lays,
And pour forth all my grateful heart in praise.
   In lifeless strains let vulgar satire tell
That marriage oft is mixed with heaven and hell,
That conjugal delight is soured with spleen,
And peace and war compose the varied scene.
My muse a truth sublimer can assert,
And sing the triumphs of a mutual heart.

Thrice happy they who through life's varied tide
With equal pace and gentle motion glide,
Whom, though the wave of fortune sinks or swells,
One reason governs and one wish impels,
Whose emulation is to love the best,
Who feels no bliss but in each other blest,
Who knows no pleasure but the joys they give,
Nor cease to love but when they cease to live.
If fate these blessings in one lot combine,
Then let th' eternal page record them mine.

Thomas Blacklock (1721–91)

The Nature of Love

Tonight

Tonight you are a hundred miles away
and I could read perhaps, or watch TV –
that serial of water, screen of fog.
I think I'd rather hold a dialogue
after the fading routine of the day
in the midnight's darkness, in the midnight's mercy.

O what is love? philosophers have asked
and more than these, the poets, What is love?
Gather your roses while the weather's good.
Love is perhaps a similar attitude
struck by two people. Love is a gay mask.
Love is constructed from a coat or glove.

Love is a mirror lined by sweet bouquets.
It is the purest vanity we know.
It is a loss of self, as saints have taught.
Love is an article that can't be bought
in shop or supermarket. Love has days
that melt to rain after a trembling rainbow.

Love can move the sun and the other stars,
absolves the golden serpent. Is the true
colour of being. Is the finest chain.
Love's the most piercing and inventive pain.
For love we suffer profound ignorant scars.
For love we soldier, and love honour too.

... The night is quiet. There's light upon the ice.
I hear your step a hundred miles away.
Accidents can happen to the soul.
Wherever we are our hearts are both at school

and suffer and enjoy not once but twice
in the blue constant weather, in the grey.

If you are Taurus and I Capricorn
astrologers and horoscopes commend
each to the other in a thrifty marriage
by the sharp rays of prudence and courage
and by each present we can truly earn –
to us the stars don't prodigally bend.

Love is incessant climbing to far peaks,
ambitious haunting. That is why I hear
your steps so clearly, miles and miles away
as if they moved in jealousy or envy –
you hack steps out with an uncertain axe
in a harsh and vast breathless atmosphere

where all is lost that isn't gained each hour.
I think, quiet Midnight, that the sun will rise
but do not know it. Therefore let my sight
not fade tonight but seem to bring the light –
and her – to my warm house, for your black air
is part of morning's and her shaking guise.

Iain Crichton Smith (b. 1928)

A Rondel of Luve

Lo! what it is to lufe,
  Lerne ye, that list to prufe,
Be me, I say, that no wayis may
  The grund of greif remufe,
Bot still decay, both nycht and day:
  Lo! what it is to lufe.

Lufe is ane fervent fyre,
  Kendillit without desyre:
Schort plesour, lang displesour;
  Repentence is the hyre;
Ane pure tressour without mesour:
  Lufe is ane fervent fyre.

To lufe and to be wyiss,
  To rege with gud advyiss,
Now thus, now than, so gois the game,
  Incertane is the dyiss:
Thair is no man, I say, that can
  Both lufe and to be wyiss.

Flee alwayis frome the snair;
  Lerne at me to be ware;
It is pane and dowbill trane
  Of endless wo and cair;
For to refrane that denger plane,
  Flee alwayis frome the snair.

Alexander Scott (c. 1520–c. 1590)

dyiss = dice

The Point of Love

What does it mean to be born?
Only a few substantial flips around the sun?
Only dependence on one star in infinity?
Only a second in a larger century?
Only a fraction of the omnipotent One?

Or the instigation of a passionate affair.
Or the reason for the beauty of her hair.
Or the centre of her particular universe.
Or the one that makes our death seem less fierce.
Or the deadly enemy of her despair.

But what if she is only human flesh
Destined to decay, to fly only to crash?
Only one in millions, a pointless whim
Of fate, a trick of carbon, an evanescent flame?
A remnant of the sentiment we have to smash?

Or the very point of staying alive
In a place so viciously combative.
Or the stimulation of the brain
Or the one who makes your life your own again
Or the entity that in herself defines love.

Alan Bold (b. 1943)

From the French

It chanced that Cupid on a season
    By Fancy urged, resolved to wed,
But could not settle whether Reason
    Or Folly should partake his bed.

What does he then? – Upon my life,
    'Twas bad example for a deity
He takes me Reason for a wife,
    And Folly for his hours of gaiety.

Though thus he dealt in petty treason,
    He loved them both in equal measure;
Fidelity was born of Reason,
    And Folly brought to bed of Pleasure.

                Sir Walter Scott (1771–1832)

from Lord of the Mirrors

A dance Bernard of Ventadour made, with masks and lutes
and ladies, for the investiture of Philip Count of Narbonne
in April 1130.

    The new prince goes among roses, cupids, peacocks.

        Beast, what is love?
        Phallus, rut, spasm.

        Peasant, what is love?
        Plough, furrow, seed.

        Priest, what is love?
        Prophecy, event, ritual.

Lord, what is love?
Lys, and daunce, and viol.

Man, what is love?
On the garden pool breezes, a
  caul of sackcloth.

George Mackay Brown (b. 1921)

To X

Not because your body is lovely or your hair,
Nor those wombs of light where love suffers openly,
Nor only for the sphere our bodies make at night,
Though these contribute, dear, and flow toward.

But because of the tears and our human needs,
Because we met in the dark and bred a flame
That kindled in the ribs of each, though never together,
Fires that joined light across the seas that severed.

Because love is not ours to command or commend
But a wreath of fulfilment offering us
Ourselves through the gift of surrender:
Not to be treated coldly ever but made at home.

And because the heart mumbling over its isolation
Rehearses death in desiring all its fears
Till love unlocks its tethered floods
Unfolding slowly the humble mother and compasses.

Tom Scott (b. 1917)

The Day the Weather Broke

Last out in the raining weather, a girl and I
drip in the splintered light while cars slur by,
and the single drizzling reason
of rain in an alien season
turns us to each other till a train arrives
to share, by bond of wetness, our wet lives.

Although at first we can find to put our thumb on
only the rain in common,
is this not what love is? That we draw together
in the inhuman weather,
strangers, who pool our sheltered selves and take,
for the gray heavens' sake,
this luck, caught without our usual cloak
the day the weather broke?

Alastair Reid (b. 1926)

No You

No you can't
have a close-circuit television
showing a brothel of all-blond negresses/
No you can't
pee and expect wine even if you are drunk/
No you can't see my heart/
No you can't
be allowed to come here with flowers
even if you do love me/
No I won't have you
invite Dr Christian Barnard to my next

birthday party, I see through you,
and you won't get to my heart that way/
No don't think I'll let you
away with writing letters on condition
that you stay in Naples
while I research the correspondence
of Thomas Carlyle/
No you can't see
the proofs, they're confidential/
No you can't,
the executors have an embargo on their love
letters, no you can't just/
you don't think you can simply/
you surely don't imagine/
You're not just going/
to catch that bus, are you?

Robert Tait (b. 1943)

Poem Before Birth

Rising from bed
I shaved. Outside, the birds awoke
And sang in pleasure through the rising mist
With bells and cars. Then something turned and spoke
Inside my borrowed head
These words that follow, and were found. Light kissed

The ploughland, white
With naked scythes. If it was Love,
Or what I wanted to believe was that,

I hardly knew then. But in air, above
    The sparrow's broken flight,
Returning from his nightlong hunt, the cat

    Saw the fine day
  And mewed for joy. I heard, and shared
His bleat of praise. As others rose, and made
The old wood flustered, as if it, too, cared
    Throughout your house, I say
I never knew how far Love was obeyed.

    The clock's low snore
  Resounded in its brazen frame
To help the time. The wind made fastened leaves
Turn in the larches. And the cherished flame
    That fell in ash before
The gathering of darkness, clasped in sheaves

    Like wheat. The chair
  I sat in seemed to flower, and snow
To roses with a scent. Inside my throat
The wine of our good meal began to slow
    And wake to vineyards. Bare
In my new body's fort, I touched the moat

    Round my content
  And felt in love. So I wrote out
At peace, and for my pleasure, these few words
To thank my evening host. Here, never doubt,
    I have to say, in scent
Of burning pine, to touch the air with birds,

    Joy comes. Today
  So honoured by the care of friends
I rise to feel safe. And when the time begins

And nothing but the emptying cellar ends
    With breakfast, and the way
Towards another room, life moves on fins

    In water, child
    Swimming to birth. So I, who praise
My lodging in a doctor's house, approve
Ceremonies of beneficence. That blaze
    Along your windows, wild
As what went hunting all night long, was Love.

George MacBeth (b. 1932)

The Circle

A circle is my love, and all
my words along that line will tell
the radius my passions fill.

You lie within it. Gently there
you nestle in its humming care,
until its humming fills your ear.

Yes, I, who spin around you, make
a universe beyond the lake,
the silent lake which is your heart.

Its depth I am, circumference round,
and moving ripples when your hand
leans out to touch me on the ground.

And yet, and yet, it is, my dear,
your stillness, not my turning here,
that makes the circle true entire.

Alan Riddell (b. 1927)

Obsessions

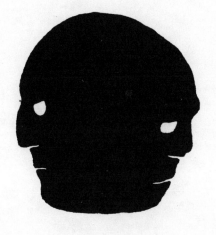

Tam i' the Kirk

O Jean, my Jean, when the bell ca's the congregation
O'er valley an' hill wi' the ding frae its iron mou',
When a'body's thochts is set on their ain salvation,
        Mine's set on you.

There's a reid rose lies on the Buik o' the Word afore ye
That was growin' braw on its bush at the keek o' day,
But the lad that pu'd yon flower i' the mornin's glory —
        He canna pray.

He canna pray, but there's nane i' the kirk will heed him
Whaur he sits sae still his lane at the side o' the wa',
For nane but the reid rose kens what my lassie gied him —
        It and us twa.

He canna sing for the sang that his ain he'rt raises,
He canna see for the mist that's afore his e'en,
And a voice drouns the hale o' the psalms an' the paraphrases,
        Crying 'Jean! Jean! Jean!'

                      Violet Jacob (1863–1947)

And Our Gifts to the Seasons

    he went out
        the snow was hard packed
        stale

    'to be unmoved'
        he thought
    the wind blew everything

in its path
'to be unmoved'

there was a summer
    lilies grew
    in great profusion
he lay down along the bank
    and she lay also
    they listened
    to the water to their own
    silence
'let me come in to you'
lilies moving on the bank

the road now
    out of town
was difficult
picking one's way
    in the deep snow
'there was a time
    I'd have turned from
    this senseless ordinance'
but no return

    the sleigh was there
    he felt
    that dark strength flowing
    from the horses

    (he heard her laugh)

and his the only footprints
    traced upon the snow

Thomas Clark (b. 1944)

Sang

There's a reid lowe in yer cheek,
Mither, and a licht in yer ee,
And ye sing like the shuilfie in the slae,
But no' for me.

The man that cam' the day,
Mither, that ye ran to meet,
He drapt his gun and fondlet ye
And I was left to greet.

Ye served him kail frae the pat,
Mither, and meat frae the bane.
Ye brocht him cherries frae the gean,
And I gat haurdly ane.

And noo he lies in yer bed,
Mither, and the licht grows dim,
And the sang ye sing as ye hap me ower
Is meant for him.

Robert McLellan (b. 1907)

lowe = flame   shuilfie = chaffinch
kail = cabbage soup   greet = weep
gean = wild cherry-tree

from *The Buik of Alexander*

When I see hir forrow me,
that is fulfillit of all bounte,
and I behald hir colour cleir,
hir hare, that to fine gold is feir,
hir cheke, hir chin, hir middle small,
hir fare-hede and her fassoun all,
I am sa movit throw that sicht
that I have nouther strenth nor micht
to heir, to see, na yit to fele.
As man suld de, this wait I wele,
thus am I staid before that fre,
for hir that all my lufe suld be.

Anon.

forrow = in front of   wait I wele = know I well
feir = companion   staid = beset
fare-hede = beauty   fre = lady
de = die

Cupid and Venus

Fra banc to banc, fra wod to wod, I rin
Ourhailit with my feble fantasie,
Lyc til a leif that fallis from a trie
Or til a reid ourblawin with the wind.
Twa gods gyds me: the ane of tham is blind,
Ye, and a bairn brocht up in vanitie;
The nixt a wyf ingenrit of the se,
And lichter nor a dauphin with hir fin.

ourhailit = overwhelmed

Unhappie is the man for evirmaire
That teils the sand and sawis in the air;
Bot twyse unhappier is he, I lairn,
That feidis in his hairt a mad desyre,
And follows on a woman throw the fyre,
Led be a blind and teichit be a bairn.

Mark Alexander Boyd (1563–1610)

teils = tills

The Mandrake Hairt

Ye saw't floueran in my breist
– My mandrake hairt –
And, wi a wild wae look
(O my dear luve!)
Ye reift it screichan out ...
And the bluid rins aye frae the torn ruit.

Sydney Goodsir Smith (1915–75)

The Grave of Love

The auld sangs soored and cankered,
Ill dreams that kept me fleyed, –
Let's get a michty coffin,
And stow them a' inside.

121

There's muckle I maun lay there,
Though what I daurna tell;
The coffin may be bigger
Than St. Andrews' auld draw-well.

And bring a bier well-timbered,
O' brods baith lang and wide:
Needs be they maun be longer
Than the auld brig ower the Clyde.

And bring me twal' great giants,
A' men o' muckle worth –
As strang as William Wallace
That looks across the Forth.

And they maun tak' the coffin
And sink it in the wave,
For sic a michty coffin
Maun hae a michty grave.

D'ye ken what way the coffin
Maun be sae great and strang?
It's my love I mean to lay there,
And the dule I've tholed so lang.

Alexander Gray (1882–1962)
trans. from Heine's *Die Alten Bosen Lieder*

My Trewth is Plicht

My trewth is plicht unto my lufe benyng
that meit and sleip is quyt bereft me fro.
With luvaris mo of murnyng I may sing
without glaidnes, whair evir I ryd or go.
And I hir freind, why suld scho be my fo?
Do as scho list, I do me in hir cure
on to the deid to be hir serviture.

And thocht I dar nocht daly do present
hir for to serf for hurting of hir name,
I dreid the serpent sklander do hir schent.
Bot nevirtheles hir honour and hir fame
I sall keip in armis and in game
unto the time that Atropus the threid
sall cute of life bayth in word and deid.

O Cupeid king, thyn eiris now incline,
and pers my lady inward to the hairt
with that ilk dart that thou hes persit mine,
and caus hir so that scho to me revarte
for to haif mercy unto my pane and smarte,
or feill the pine that faithfull luvaris haif,
for, but hir lufe, I graith me to my graif.

Sir John Fethy (?1480–c. 1570)

do hir schent = ruin her   graith me = prepare myself

O, were I on Parnassus Hill

O were I on Parnassus hill,
Or had o' Helicon my fill,
That I might catch poetic skill,
   To sing how dear I love thee!
But Nith maun be my Muse's well,
My muse maun be thy bonie sel':
On Corsincon I'll glowr and spell,
   And write how dear I love thee!

Then come, sweet Muse, inspire my lay!
For a' the lee-lang simmer's day,
I couldna sing, I couldna say,
   How much, how dear, I love thee.
I see thee dancing o'er the green –
Thy waist sae jimp, thy limbs sae clean
Thy tempting lips, thy roguish een, –
   By Heaven and earth I love thee!

By night, by day, a-field, at hame,
The thoughts o' thee my breast inflame;
And ay I muse and sing thy name,
   I only live to love thee.
Tho' I were doom'd to wander on,
Beyond the sea, beyond the sun;
Till my last, weary sand was run, –
   Till then – and then I love thee!

Robert Burns (1759–96)

Continent o Venus

She lies ablow my body's lust and love,
A country dearly-kent, and yet sae fremd
That she's at aince thon Tir-nan-Og I've dreamed,
The airt I've lived in, whar I mean tae live,
And mair, much mair, a mixter-maxter world
Whar fact and dream are taigled up and snorled.

I ken ilk bay o aa her body's strand,
Yet ken them new ilk time I come to shore,
For she's the uncharted sea whar I maun fare
To find anither undiscovered land,
To find it fremd, and yet to find it dear,
To seek it aye, and aye be bydan there.

Alexander Scott (b. 1920)

fremd = foreign   Tir-nan-Og = land of youth, Gaelic
paradise

Woman's Faith

Woman's faith, and woman's trust –
Write the characters in dust;
Stamp them on the running stream,
Print them on the moon's pale beam,
And each evanescent letter
Shall be clearer, firmer, better,
And more permanent, I ween,
Than the thing those letters mean.

I have strain'd the spider's thread
'Gainst the promise of a maid;
I have weigh'd a grain of sand
'Gainst her plight of heart and hand;
I told my true love of the token,
How her faith proved light, and her
    word was broken:
Again her word and truth she plight,
And I believed them again ere night.

Sir Walter Scott (1771–1832)

Warnings

The Unquiet Grave

'The wind doth blow to-day, my love,
   And a few small drops of rain;
I never had but one true-love;
   In cold grave she was lain.

'I'll do as much for my true-love
   As any young man may;
I'll sit and mourn all at her grave
   For a twelvemonth and a day.'

The twelvemonth and a day being up,
   The dead began to speak:
'Oh, who sits weeping on my grave,
   And will not let me sleep?'

' 'T is I, my love, sits on your grave,
   And will not let you sleep;
For I crave one kiss of your clay-cold lips,
   And that is all I seek.'

'You crave one kiss of my clay-cold lips;
   But my breath smells earthy strong;
If you have one kiss of my clay-cold lips,
   Your time will not be long.

' 'T is down in yonder garden green,
   Love, where we used to walk,
The finest flower that ere was seen
   Is wither'd to a stalk.

'The stalk is wither'd dry, my love,
   So will our hearts decay;

So make yourself content, my love,
Till God calls you away.'

Anon.

A Ballad of Orpheus

On the third day after her unexpected death,
Orpheus descended into Hell.
It wasn't hard to find. He knew the directions well;
asleep, he'd often read them by the light of his own breath.

The doorkeeper was surly, but let him in;
he had no reason to keep anyone out.
Glaring like a lit city, a kind of visible shout
fungused about the place, an absolute din

of all notes, overtones and unheard sounds at once.
To keep his sense of self intact, he struck
a few familiar chords, and as his luck
would have it, she, who all along had felt a hunch

something unusual would happen, heard the order
and limiting purpose of his playing; and being not yet
fully subtracted out of herself to fit
Hell's edgeless ambiguities, broke from the border

of blurring dissolution, and moved towards her lover
as a cloud might move in the world of gods above.
He guessed that shape and stir to be his love
Eurydice, well knowing that no other

130

idea of woman would answer to the lyre
that sang against his loins. She came to him crying
aloud her numbed womanly tenderness, trying
to warm her cold half-body at the core of his fire.

But without a word said, he seized her hand
and began pulling her roughly along the road,
past the doorkeeper, who smirked, seeing the load
he carried. She, being woman couldn't understand

that love in action needs no drag of speech,
and pled with him to turn round once and kiss
her. Of all the conditions the gods had imposed, this
was the one he dared not disobey. Reproach

followed reproach; till, as he fled
through shadow to shadow, suddenly it seemed
that the only absolute good was what he'd dreamed
of her. So Orpheus stopped, and slowly turned his head.

At once she began to small. He watched her disappear
backwards from him, and thought it best
that things should be so. How could he have stood the test
of constant loving, always with the fear

of his first loss ahead of him again,
believing happiness ends in boredom or pain?
So Orpheus returned by the same lane
as he went down by, to compose himself in a world of men.

But there's a sequel to this traveller's tale.
The Thracian women, sensing the need to purge
his unfulfilment of the sexual urge,
tore his manhood apart, and with a wail

that made even Hell's distant doorkeeper tremble,
threw his warm parts onto the legendary floods.
The warning here to all you whole young bloods
who go out after women is: don't dissemble.

Maurice Lindsay (b. 1918)

from The Queen's Wake

The Song

'O! Lady dear, fair is thy noon,
But man is like the inconstant moon:
Last night she smiled o'er lawn and lea;
That moon will change, and so will he.

'Thy time, dear Lady, 's a passing shower;
Thy beauty is but a fading flower;
Watch thy young bosom, and maiden eye,
For the shower must fall, and the flow'ret die.'

What ails my Queen? said good Argyle,
Why fades upon her cheek the smile?
Say, rears your steed too fierce and high?
Or sits your golden seat awry?

. . . .

Queen Mary lighted in the court;
Queen Mary joined the evening's sport;
Yet though at table all were seen,
To wonder at her air and mien;

Though courtiers fawned and ladies sung,
Still in her ear the accents rung, –
'Watch thy young bosom, and maiden eye,
'For the shower must fall, and the flowret die.'
These words prophetic seemed to be,
Foreboding wo and misery;
And much she wished to prove ere long,
The wonderous powers of Scottish song.

James Hogg (1770-1835)

To a Very Beautiful Lady

And when you walk the world lifts up its head,
Planets are haloed by the unembarrassed stars,
The town lies fallow at your feet, the ancient dead
Recall their loves, their queens and emperors,
Their shepherds and the quiet pastoral scene.
For less than you Troy burned and Egypt fell,
The corn was blasted while it still stood green,
And Faustus went protesting into Hell.

Be careful, sweet, adored by half the world,
Time to its darlings is not always kind,
There lie the lovelies whom the years have scored
Deeper than all the hearts which once repined.
The knife you hold could cut an empire low
Or in your own breast place the suicidal blow.

Ruthven Todd (1914–1978)

Sonnet 26

Ile give thee leave my love, in beauties field
To reare red colours whiles, and bend thine eyes;
Those that are bashfull still, I quite despise
Such simple soules are too soone mov'd to yeeld:
Let majestie arm'd in thy count'nance sit,
As that which will no injurie receive;
And Ile not hate thee, whiles although thou have
A sparke of pride, so it be rul'd by wit.
This is to chastitie a powerfull guard,
Whil'st haughtie thoughts all servile things eschue,
That sparke hath power the passions to subdue,
And would of glorie chalenge a reward:
    But do not fall in love with thine owne selfe;
    Narcissus earst was lost on such a shelfe.

Sir William Alexander, Earl of Stirling (1567–1640)

whiles = sometimes
earst = formerly

Thread

If I love you
Your life instantly becomes
More fragile than my own,
Your body more frail
Each cough or minor pain
A symptom of some dread
Disease or other.

Death is on every road
Or in every other car
Some nights in my skin
Flutters in apprehension
And I am so threatened that
Caring translates itself
Inside my head to
Stone cold anger.

Because I am unsufficient
Tormented by the frailty
Of you whom I love.
Selfish I
Find you
Necessary for my own definition
Your life is a single thread
It snaps
I wither.

Catherine Lucy Czerkawska (b. 1950)

The Shadows

'I think,' she said, 'we shall not see again
each other as we did.' The light is fading
that was once sunny in the April rain.
Across the picture there appears a shading
we didn't notice, but was in the grain.

The picture shows two people happily smiling
with their arms around each other, by the sea.
Whatever they are looking at is beguiling
themselves to themselves. There is a tree
with orange blossoms and an elegant styling

but they are lost quite clearly in each other.
They do not see the landscape, do not hear
the stream that tinkles through the azure weather.
It's as if really the clear atmosphere
were a creation of two souls together.

But at the back there steadily grow two shadows
one for each lover that they can't evade.
They emerge threateningly from the coloured meadows
as if they were a track the two had made
and they were ignorant of, their changeless natures.

And as they move the shades intently follow
growing steadily darker, spreading as they go
as the wings' shades pursue the flying swallow.
My dearest love, if these should make us slow –
remember late the first undying halo.

Iain Crichton Smith (b. 1928)

The Birks of Invermay

The smiling morn, the breathing spring,
Invite the tuneful birds to sing;
And while they warble from each spray,
Love melts the universal lay.
Let us, Amanda, timely wise,
Like them improve the hour that flies;
And in soft raptures waste the day
Among the shades of Invermay.

For soon the winter of the year,
And age, life's winter, will appear;
At this thy living bloom will fade,
As that will strip the vernal shade.
Our taste of pleasure then is o'er;
The feathered songsters love no more;
And when they droop and we decay,
Adieu the shades of Invermay!

David Mallet (1700–65)

Laments

from The Songs of Selma

Colma — It is night; I am alone, forlorn on the hill of storms. The wind is heard in the mountain. The torrent pours down the rock. No hut receives me from the rain; forlorn on the hill of winds!

Rise, moon! from behind thy clouds. Stars of the night arise! Lead me, some light, to the place where my love rests from the chace alone! His bow near him, unstrung: His dogs panting around him. But here I must sit alone, by the rock of the mossy stream. The stream and the wind roar aloud. I hear not the voice of my love! Why delays my Salgar, why the chief of the hill, his promise? Here is the roaring stream! Thou didst promise with night to be here. Ah! Whither is my Salgar gone? With thee I would fly, from my father; with thee, from my brother of pride. Our race have long been foes; we are not foes, O Salgar!

Cease a little while, O wind! Stream, be thou silent a while! Let my voice be heard around. Let my wanderer hear me! Salgar! It is Colma who calls. Here is the tree, and the rock. Salgar, my love! I am here. Why delayest thou thy coming? Lo! the calm moon comes forth. The flood is bright in the vale. The rocks are grey on the steep. I see him not on the brow. His dogs come not before him, with tidings of his near approach. Here I must sit alone!

Who lie on the heath beside me? Are they my love and my brother? Speak to me, O my friends! To Colma they give no reply. Speak to me: I am alone! My soul is tormented with fears! Ah! they are dead! Their swords are red from the fight. Oh my brother! my brother! Why hast thou slain my Salgar? Why, O Salgar, has thou slain my brother? Dear were ye both to me! What shall I say in your praise? Thou wert fair on the hill among thousands! He was terrible in fight. Speak to me; hear my voice; hear me, sons of my love! They are silent; silent for ever! Cold, cold are their breasts of clay! Oh! from the rock on the hill; from the top of the windy steep, speak, ye ghosts of the dead! I will not be afraid! Whither are you gone to rest? In what cave of the hill shall I find the departed? No feeble voice is on the gale: No answer half-drowned in the storm!

I sit in my grief! I wait for morning in my tears! Rear the tomb, ye friends of the dead. Close it not till Colma come. My life flies away like a dream: Why should I stay behind? Here shall I rest with my friends, by the stream of the founding rock. When night comes on the hill; when the loud winds arise; my ghost shall stand in the blast, and mourn the death of my friends. The hunter shall hear from his booth. He shall fear, but love my voice! For sweet shall my voice be for my friends: Pleasant were her friends to Colma!

James Macpherson (1738–96)

To a Ladye

Sweit rois of vertew and of gentilnes,
Delytsum lyllie of everie lustynes,
　　Richest in bontie and in bewtie cleir,
　　And everie vertew that is held most deir,
Except onlie that ye ar mercyles.

In to your garthe this day I did persew,
Thair saw I flowris that fresche were of hew;

garthe = garden

Baith whyte and reid moist lusty wer to seyne,
And halsum herbis upone stalkis grene;
   Yit leif nor flour fynd could I nane of rew.

I dout that Merche, with his caild blastis keyne,
Hes slane this gentill herbe that I of mene,
   Whois petewous deithe dois to my hart sic pane
   That I wald mak to plant his rute agane,
So confortand his levis unto me bene.

William Dunbar (?1456–?1513)

mene = moan

Waly, Waly

O waly, waly up the bank!
   And waly, waly, down the brae!
And waly, waly yon burn-side,
   Where I and my love wont to gae!

I lean'd my back unto an aik,
   I thought it was a trusty tree;
But first it bow'd, and syne it brak,
   Sae my true-love did lightly me.

O waly, waly! but love be bony
   A little time, while it is new;
But when 'tis auld, it waxeth cauld,
   And fades away like morning dew.

waly = woefully

143

O wherefore should I busk my head?
     Or wherefore should I kame my hair?
For my true-love has me forsook,
     And says he'll never love me mair.

Now Arthur-Seat shall be my bed,
     The sheets shall ne'er be fyl'd by me;
Saint Anton's well shall be my drink,
     Since my true-love has forsaken me.

Martinmas wind, when wilt thou blaw,
     And shake the green leaves off the tree?
O gentle death, when wilt thou come?
     For of my life I am weary.

'Tis not the frost that freezes fell,
     Nor blawing snaw's inclemency;
'Tis not sic cauld that makes me cry,
     But my love's heart grown cauld to me.

When we came in by Glasgow town,
     We were a comely sight to see;
My love was cled in the black velvet,
     And I my sell in cramasie.

But had I wist, before I kiss'd,
     That love had been sae ill to win,
I'd lock'd my heart in a case of gold,
     And pin'd it with a silver pin.

Oh, oh, if my young babe were born,
     And set upon the nurse's knee,

fyl'd = defiled   cramasie = crimson
fell = intensely

144

And I my sell were dead and gane!
For a maid again I'll never be.

Anon.

Ye Banks and Braes

Ye banks and braes o' bonie Doon,
 How can ye bloom sae fresh and fair!
How can ye chant, ye little birds,
 And I sae weary fu' o' care!
Thou'll break my heart, thou warbling bird,
 That wantons thro' the flow'ring thorn,
Thou minds me o' departed joys,
 Departed, never to return.

Oft hae I rov'd by bonie Doon,
 To see the rose and woodbine twine;
And ilka bird sang o' its Luve
 And fondly sae did I o' mine;
Wi' lightsome heart I pu'd a rose,
 Fu' sweet upon its thorny tree;
And my fause Luver staw my rose,
 But, ah! he left the thorn wi' me.

Robert Burns (1759–96)

The Flowers of the Forest

I've heard the lilting at our yowe-milking,
Lasses a-lilting before the dawn o' day;
But now they are moaning on ilka green loaning:
'The Flowers of the Forest are a' wede away.'

At buchts, in the morning, nae blythe lads are scorning;
The lasses are lonely, and dowie, and wae;
Nae daffin', nae gabbin', but sighing and sabbing:
Ilk ane lifts her leglen, and hies her away.

In hairst, at the shearing, nae youths now are jeering,
The bandsters are lyart, and runkled and grey;
At fair or at preaching, nae wooing, nae fleeching:
The Flowers of the Forest are a' wede away.

At e'en, in the gloaming, nae swankies are roaming
'Bout stacks wi' the lasses at bogle to play,
But ilk ane sits drearie, lamenting her dearie:
The Flowers of the Forest are a' wede away.

Dule and wae for the order sent our lads to the Border;
The English, for ance, by guile wan the day;
The Flowers of the Forest, that foucht aye the foremost,
The prime o' our land, are cauld in the clay.

loaning = lane	lyart = grizzled
wede = withered	fleeching = coaxing
buchts = cattle pens	swankies = young bucks
dowie = sad	bogle = peek-a-boo
daffin' = dallying	dule = grief
hairst = harvest	

We'll hear nae mair lilting at our yowe-milking;
Women and bairns are heartless and wae:
Sighing and moaning on ilka green loaning:
'The Flowers of the Forest are a' wede away.'

Jean Elliot (1727–1805)

If Langour Makis Men Licht

If langour makis men licht,
Or dolour thame decoir,
In erth thair is no wicht
May me compair in gloir.
If cairfull thochtis restoir
My havy hairt frome sorrow,
I am for evermoir
In joy both evin and morrow.

If plesour be to pance,
I playnt me nocht opprest;
Or absence micht avance,
My hairt is haill possest.
If want of quiet rest
From cairis micht me convoy,
My mind is nocht mollest,
Bot evermoir in joy.

Thocht that I pance in pane
In passing to and fro,
I laubor all in vane;

decoir = adorn	pance = think
gloir = glory	

For so hes mony mo
That hes nocht servit so
In suting of thair sueit.
The nar the fyre I go,
The grittar is my heit.

The turtour for hir maik
Mair dule may nocht indure
Nor I do for hir saik,
Evin hir wha hes in cure
My hart, whilk sal be sure
In service to the deid
Unto that lady pure,
The well of womanheid.

Schaw schedull to that sueit,
My pairt so permanent,
That no mirth whill we meit
Sall cause me be content;
Bot still my hairt lament
In sorrowfull siching soir
Till tyme scho be present.
Fairweill. I say no moir.

Henry Stewart, Lord Darnley (1545–67)

turtour = turtle dove   schedull = statement
maik = mate   whill = until
dule = sorrow

from The Widow of Glencoe

Do not lift him from The bracken,
  Leave him lying where he fell —
Better bier ye cannot fashion:
  None beseems him half so well
As the bare and broken heather,
  And the hard and trampled sod,
Whence his angry soul ascended
  To the judgement-seat of God!

         . . . .

Tremblingly we scooped the covering
  From each kindred victim's head,
And the living lips were burning
  On the cold ones of the dead.
And I left them with their dearest —
  Dearest charge had every one —
Left the maiden with her lover,
  Left the mother with her son.
I alone of all was mateless —
  Far more wretched I than they,
For the snow would not discover
  Where my Lord and husband lay.
But I wandered up the valley,
  Till I found him lying low,
With the gash upon his bosom
  And the frown upon his brow —
Till I found him lying murdered,
  Where he wooed me long ago!
Women's weakness shall not shame me
  Why should I have tears to shed?
Could I rain them down like water,
  O my hero! on thy head —

Could the cry of lamentation
    Wake thee from thy silent sleep,
Could it set thy heart a throbbing,
    It were mine to wail and weep!
But I will not waste my sorrow,
    Lest the Campbell women say
That the daughters of Clanranald
    Are as weak and frail as they.

. . . .

Other eyes than mine shall glisten,
    Other hearts be rent in twain,
Ere the heathbells on thy hillock
    Wither in the autumn rain.
Then I'll seek thee where thou sleepest,
    And I'll veil my weary head,
Praying for a place beside thee,
    Dearer than my bridal-bed:
And I'll give thee tears, my husband!
    If the tears remain to me,
When the widows of the foemen
    Cry the coronach for thee!

William Aytoun (1813-65)

Alas for Him Whose Sickness is Love

Alas for him whose sickness is love,
for what cause soever I should say it;
hard it is to be free of it;
sad is the plight in which I am myself.

That love which I have given in secret,
since it profits me to declare it not,
if I find not quick relief,
my bloom will be slight and meagre.

He to whom I have given love,
since I cannot speak it openly,
if me he should put in pain,
may himself have cause to say a hundred times, alas!

Iseabal Ní Mheic Cailéin (c. 1460) trans. from Gaelic

Unrequited Love

The Maid of Neidpath

O lovers' eyes are sharp to see,
    And lovers' ears in hearing;
And love, in life's extremity,
    Can lend an hour of cheering.
Disease had been in Mary's bower,
    And slow decay from mourning,
Though now she sits on Neidpath's Tower,
    To watch her love's returning.

All sunk and dim her eyes so bright,
    Her form decay'd by pining,
Till through her wasted hand, at night,
    You saw the taper shining;
By fits, a sultry hectic hue
    Across her cheek was flying;
By fits, so ashy pale she grew,
    Her maidens thought her dying.

Yet keenest powers to see and hear
    Seem'd in her frame residing;
Before the watch-dog prick'd his ear
    She heard her lover's riding;
Ere scarce a distant form was ken'd,
    She knew, and waved to greet him;
And o'er the battlement did bend,
    As on the wing to meet him.

He came – he pass'd – an heedless gaze,
    As o'er some stranger glancing;
Her welcome, spoke in faltering phrase,
    Lost in his courser's prancing.

The castle arch, whose hollow tone
Returns each whisper spoken,
Could scarcely catch the feeble moan
Which told her heart was broken.

Sir Walter Scott (1771–1832)

To Luve Unluvit

To luve unluvit it is ane pane;
For scho that is my soverane,
    Sum wantoun man so he hes set hir,
That I can get no lufe agane,
    Bot brekis my hairt, and nocht the bettir.

When that I went with that sweit may,
To dance, to sing, to sport and pley,
    And oft tymes in my armis plet hir;
I do now murne both nycht and day,
    And brekis my hart, and nocht the bettir.

Whair I wes wont to see hir go
Rycht trymly passand to and fro,
    With cumly smylis when that I met hir;
And now I leif in pane and wo,
    And brekis my hairt, and nocht the bettir.

Whattane ane glaikit fule am I
To slay myself with malancoly,
    Sen weill I ken I may nocht get hir!
Or what suld be the caus, and why,
    To brek my hairt, and nocht the bettir?

may = maid   plet = embraced   glaikit = silly

My hairt, sen thou may nocht hir pleiss,
Adew, as gude lufe cumis as gaiss,
  Go chuss ane udir and forget hir;
God gif him dolour and diseiss,
  That brekis thair hairt and nocht the bettir.

Finis q. Scott, When His Wyfe Left Him.

Alexander Scott (?1520–?1590)

Mary's Song

I wad ha'e gi'en him my lips tae kiss,
Had I been his, had I been his;
Barley breid and elder wine,
Had I been his as he is mine.

The wanderin' bee it seeks the rose;
Tae the lochan's bosom the burnie goes;
The grey bird cries at evenin's fa',
'My luve, my fair one, come awa'.'

My beloved sall ha'e this he'rt tae break,
Reid, reid wine and the barley cake,
A he'rt tae break, an' a mou' tae kiss,
Tho' he be nae mine, as I am his.

Marion Angus (1866–1946)

Earl Richard

Earl Richard is a hunting gone,
  As fast as he can ride,
His hunting-horn hung about his neck,
  And a small sword by his side.

When he came to my lady's gate
  He tirled at the pin,
And wha was sae ready as the lady hersell
  To open and let him in.

'O light, O light, Earl Richard,' she says,
  'O light and stay a' night;
You shall have cheer wi charcoal clear,
  And candles burning bright.'

'I will not light, I cannot light,
  I cannot light at all;
A fairer lady than ten of thee
  Is waiting at Richard's Wall.'

He stooped from his milk-white steed,
  To kiss her rosy cheek;
She had a pen-knife in her hand,
  And wounded him so deep.

'O lie ye there, Earl Richard,' she says,
  'O lie ye there till morn;
A fairer lady than ten of me
  Will think lang of your coming home.'

She called her servants ane by ane,
  She called them twa by twa:

'I have got a dead man in my bower,
    I wish he were awa.'

The one has taen him by the hand,
    And the other by the feet,
And they've thrown him in a deep draw-well,
    Full fifty fathom deep.

Then up bespake a little bird,
    That sat upon a tree:
'Gae hame, gae hame, ye false lady,
    And pay your maids their fee.'

'Come down, come down, my pretty bird,
    That sits upon the tree;
I have a cage of beaten gold,
    I'll gie it unto thee.'

'Gae hame, gae hame, ye fause lady,
    And pay your maids their fee;
As ye have done to Earl Richard,
    Sae wud ye do to me.'

'If I had an arrow in my hand,
    And a bow bent on a string,
I'd shoot a dart at thy proud heart,
    Amang the leaves sae green.'

Anon.

To Minnie
(with a Hand-glass)

A picture-frame for you to fill,
   A paltry setting for your face,
A thing that has no worth until
   You lend it something of your grace,

I send (unhappy I that sing
   Laid by awhile upon the shelf)
Because I would not send a thing
   Less charming than you are yourself.

And happier than I, alas!
   (Dumb thing, I envy its delight)
'Twill wish you well, the looking-glass,
   And look you in the face to-night.

           Robert Louis Stevenson (1850–94)

from The Lord of the Isles

No! sum thine Edith's wretched lot
In these brief words. He loves her not.

           Sir Walter Scott (1771–1832)

Fainthearts

Diane

Tired and dejected hair dripping
wet trying to hitch a ride
up Loch Lomondside. Her mini
stops short, a shaking wheezing
white terrier. I stare in
surprise I've waited nearly four
hours for this moment. 'Cumonn.
Gerrin.' She drawls we jerk
off and smash puddles northwards.

'Road's crawling with bloody
hitchers' she complains, 'but
I liked the tired way you
smiled.' We talk, she teaches
poetry in Australia, I read
her some of mine, she's impressed.
Wow! The gorgeous doll's impressed!

Tired now but laughing still
we tumble over to Skye
I fall asleep and talk
all night she listens
and cackles evilly into
her cornflakes tantalising
me with what I might
or might not have said.

Then out on the road to laugh
uproariously round the island
the car barking and yelping
with glee cocking its leg
at passing places nipping the
heels of lumbering buses. Screech

of brakes and out she leaps
sprinting up the drunken
road sandals flapping bangles
clinking mad hoops flying
round her pants. 'You crazy
kite you can't catch sheep!
It's not allowed!' Chokes back
into the driving seat 'I only
wanted to FEEL him!'

Zoom back to the caravan
fling her psychedelic suitcase
into the panting car. Swop
'phone numbers – world apart
yet nearer than that. A last
whoop of laughter as she unleashes
the mini and they chase bumble
bees to the ferry together. Some
times I wish I'd kissed her.

Stewart McIntosh (b. 1948)

May Poem

When Flora had ourfret the firth
In May, of every moneth quene,
When merle and mavis singis with mirth,
Sweit melling in the schawis schene,

ourfret = adorned   melling = mingling
firth = wood   schawis = groves
merle = blackbird   schene = bright
mavis = thrush

When all luvaris rejosit bene,
And most desyrus of thair pray,
I hard a lusty luvar mene,
'I luve, bot I dar nocht assay.

Strang ar the panis I daylie prufe,
Bot yit with pacience I sustene,
I am so fetterit with the lufe
Onlie of my lady schene,
Whilk for hir bewty mycht be quene,
Natour so craftely alwey
Hes done depaint that sweit serene:
Whome I luf, I dar nocht assay.

Scho is so brycht of hyd and hew,
I lufe bot hir allone, I wene;
Is non hir luf that may eschew
That blenkis of that dulce amene,
So cumly cleir ar hir twa ene,
That scho ma luvaris dois effrey
Than evir of Grice did fair Helene;
Whom I luve, I dar nocht assay.'

Anon. (c. 1500)

mene = moan   amene = pleasant
serene = siren   ma = more
wene = conjecture   effrey = affright
blenkis = glances

Fane Wald I Luve

Fane wald I luve, bot whair about?
Thair is so mony luvaris thairout
That thair is left no place to me;
Whairof I hovit now in dout,
If I sould luve or lat it be.

Sa mony ar, their ladeis treitis
With triumphand amoures balleitis,
And dois thair bewteis pryis so he,
That I find not bot daft consaitis
To say of luve. Bot lat it be.

Sum thinkis his lady lustiest;
Sum haldis his lady for the best;
Sum sayis his luve is A *per se*;
Bot sum forsuth ar so opprest
With luve, wer bettir lat it be.

Sum for his ladyis luve lyis seik,
Suppois scho comptis it not a leik,
And sum droupis doun as he wold die;
Sum strykis doun a threid-bair cheik
For luve, war bettir lat it be.

Sum luvis lang and lyis behind;
Sum luvis and freindschip can not fynd;
Sum festnit is and ma not flee;
Sum led is lyk the belly blynd
With luve, wer bettir lat it be.

Thocht luve be grene in gud curage,
And be difficill till assuage,

hovit = remained   treitis = entreat

The end of it is miserie.
Misgovernit youth makis gowsty age.
Forbeir ye not, and lat it be.

Bot wha perfytly wald imprent,
Sould fynd his luve moist permanent;
Luve God, thy prince, and friend, all three;
Treit weill thyself and stand content,
And latt all uthir luvaris be.

(?John) Clerk (? before 1500)

gowsty = dreamy   imprent = impress

Werena My Heart Licht

There was ance a may, and she lo'ed na men;
She biggit her bonnie bow'r doun i' yon glen;
But now she cries dule and a well-a-day!
Come doun the green gate and come here away.

When bonnie young Johnnie cam' ower the sea
He said he saw naething sae bonnie as me;
He hecht me baith rings and monie braw things;
And werena my heart licht I wad dee.

He had a wee tittie that lo'ed na me,
Because I was twice as bonnie as she;
She raised sic a pother 'twixt him and his mother,
That werena my heart licht I wad dee.

biggit = built   hecht = promised
gate = way   tittie = sister

167

The day it was set and the bridal to be –
The wife took a dwam and lay doun to dee;
She maned, and she graned, out o' dolour and pain,
Till he vowed that he ne'er wad see me again.

His kin was for ane o' a higher degree,
Said, what had he to do wi' the like o' me?
Albeit I was bonnie, I wasna for Johnnie:
And werena my heart licht I wad dee.

They said I had neither cow nor calf,
Nor dribbles o' drink rins through the draff,
Nor pickles o' meal rins through the mill-e'e;
And werena my heart licht I wad dee.

His tittie she was baith wily and slee,
She spied me as I cam' ower the lea,
And then she ran in and made a loud din;
Believe your ain een an ye trow na me.

His bannet stood aye fu' round on his brow –
His auld ane looked aye as weel as some's new;
But now he lets't wear ony gate it will hing,
And casts himsel' dowie upon the corn-bing.

And now he gaes drooping about the dykes
And a' he dow do is to hund the tykes;
The love-lang nicht he ne'er steeks his e'e;
And werena my heart licht I wad dee.

dwam = swoon   dow = can
draff = grain   steeks = closes

Were I young for thee as I ha'e been
We should ha'e been gallopin' doun on yon green,
And linkin' it on the lily-white lea;
And wow gin I were but young for thee.

Lady Grizel Baillie (1665–1746)

linkin' it = going arm in arm

Love is Like a Dizziness

Chorus

O, Love, love, love!
Love is like a dizziness;
It winna let a poor body
Gang about his biziness!

James Hogg (1770–1835)

The Baffled Knight

There was a knight, and he was young,
A riding along the way, sir,
And there he met a lady fair,
Among the cocks of hay, sir.

Quoth he, Shall you and I, lady,
Among the grass lye down a?

And I will have a special care
    Of rumpling of your gown a.

'If you will go along with me
    Unto my father's hall, sir,
You shall enjoy my maidenhead,
    And my estate and all, sir.'

So he mounted her on a milk-white steed,
    Himself upon another,
And then they rid upon the road,
    Like sister and like brother.

And when she came to her father's house,
    Which was moated round about, sir,
She stepped streight within the gate,
    And shut this young knight out, sir.

'Here is a purse of gold,' she said,
    'Take it for your pains, sir;
And I will send my father's man
    To go home with you again, sir.

'And if you meet a lady fair,
    As you go thro the next town, sir,
You must not fear the dew of the grass,
    Nor the rumpling of her gown, sir.

'And if you meet a lady gay,
    As you go by the hill, sir,
If you will not when you may,
    You shall not when you will, sir.'

Anon.

Doomed Love

The Constant North

Encompass me, my lover,
With your eyes' wide calm.
Though noonday shadows are assembling doom,
The sun remains when I remember them;
And death, if it should come,
Must fall like quiet snow from such clear skies.

Minutes we snatched from the unkind winds
Are grown into daffodils by the sea's
Edge, mocking its green miseries;
Yet I seek you hourly still, over
A new Atlantis loneliness, blind
As a restless needle held by the constant north we
    always have in mind.

                  J. F. Hendry (1912–1986)

Lancelot's Soliloquy in Prison
from *Lancelot of the Laik*

What have I gilt, allace! or what deservit,
that thus mine hart shal wondit ben and carvit
one by the sword of double peine and wo?
My comfort and my plesans is ago:
to me is nat that shuld me glaid reservit.

I curs the time of mine Nativitee,
Whar in the heven it ordinyd was for me

gilt = guilt   ago = gone

173

in all my lyve never til have ees,
but for to be example of dises:
and that apperith that every wicht may see.

Sen thelke time that I had sufficians
of age, and chargit thoghtis sufferans,
nor never I continewite haith o day
without the payne of thoghtis hard assay:
thus goith my youth in tempest and penans.

And now my body is in presone broght;
but of my wo, that in regard is noght,
the wich mine hart felith ever more.
O deth, allace! why hath you me forbore
that of remed haith thee so long besoght!

Anon. (c. 1475)

thelke = that same   continewite haith = (had) a
chargit = heavy   single continuous

Lord Randal

'O where hae ye been, Lord Randal, my son?
O where hae ye been, my handsome young man?'
'I hae been to the wild wood; mother, make my bed soon,
For I'm weary wi' hunting, and fain wald lie down.'

'Where gat ye your dinner, Lord Randal, my son?
Where gat ye your dinner, my handsome young man?'
'I din'd wi' my true-love; mother, make my bed soon,
For I'm weary wi' hunting, and fain wald lie down.'

'What gat ye to your dinner, Lord Randal, my son?
What gat ye to your dinner, my handsome young man?'
'I gat eels boil'd in broo; mother, make my bed soon,
For I'm weary wi' hunting, and fain wald lie down.'

'What became of your bloodhounds, Lord Randal, my son?
What became of your bloodhounds, my handsome young
    man?'
'O they swell'd and they died; mother, make my bed soon,
For I'm weary wi' hunting, and fain wald lie down.'

'O I fear ye are poison'd, Lord Randal, my son!
O I fear ye are poison'd, my handsome young man!'
'O yes! I am poison'd; mother, make my bed soon,
For I'm sick at the heart, and I fain wald lie down.'

Anon.

The Moon Was A-waning

The moon was a-waning,
    The tempest was over;
Fair was the maiden,
    And fond was the lover;
But the snow was so deep,
    That his heart it grew weary,
And he sunk down to sleep,
    In the moorland so dreary.

Soft was the bed
    She had made for her lover,
White were the sheets
    And embroider'd the cover;

But his sheets are more white,
    And his canopy grander,
And sounder he sleeps
    Where the hill foxes wander.

Alas, pretty maiden,
    What sorrows attend you!
I see you sit shivering,
    With lights at your window;
But long may you wait
    Ere your arms shall enclose him,
For still, still he lies,
    With a wreath on his bosom!

How painful the task
    The sad tidings to tell you! –
An orphan you were
    Ere this misery befell you;
And far in yon wild,
    Where the dead-tapers hover,
So cold, cold and wan
    Lies the corpse of your lover!

James Hogg (1770–1835)

Clerk Saunders

An ensign and a lady gay,
    As they were walking on a green,
The ensign said to the lady gay,
    Will you tak me to your bower at een?

'I have seven bluidy brithers,
    Och and to you they have nae good will;
And if they catch you in my bower,
    They'll value not your bluid to spill.'

'O you may take me on your back,
    And carry me to your chamber-bed,
That I may swear, and avow richt clear,
    That your flowery bower I did never tread.

'O take a napkin from your pocket,
    And with it blindfold my een,
That I may swear, and avow richt clear,
    That your flowery bower I have never seen.'

O she's taen him upon her back,
    And carried him to her chamber-bed,
That he might swear, and avow it clear,
    That her flowery bower he did never tread.

O she's taen a napkin from her pocket,
    And with it blinded baith his een,
That he might swear, and avow it clear,
    That her flowery bower he had never seen.

They were not well into their bed,
    Nor were they scarsely fallen asleep,
Till in there came her seven bluidy brithers,
    And placed themselves at the ensign's feet.

Said the first one to the second,
    'Och it is long since this love began;'
Said the second unto the third,
    'It's a sin to kill a sleeping man.'

Said the third one to the fourth,
  'I will go to yon tavern hie;'
Said the fourth one to the fifth,
  'O if you will go, so will I.'

Said the fifth to the sixth,
  'Och it's long since this love began;'
Said the sixth to the seventh,
  'It's a sin to kill a sleeping man.'

Out then spoke the seventh bluidy brither,
  Aye and an angry man was he:
'Altho there was no more men alive,
  The ensign's butcher I will be.'

He's taen out his rusty broad-sword,
  And ran it three times along his throat,
And thro and thro the ensign's body
  The tempered steel it went thro and thro.

'O I have dreamed a dream,' she said,
  'And such an dreams cannot be good;
I dreamed my bower was full of swine,
  And the ensign's clothes all dipped in blood.

'I have dreamed another dream,
  And such an dreams are never good;
That I was combing down my yellow hair,
  And dipping it in the ensign's blood.'

'O hold your tongue, my sister dear,
  And of your weeping let a be;
For I will get you a better match
  Than eer the ensign, what was he?'

'So woe be to you, my seven bluidy brithers,
  Aye and an ill death may you die!
For you durst not fight him in battle-field,
  But you killed him sleeping in bed wi me.

'I'll do more for my love's sake
  That other lovers would not incline;
Seven years shall come and go
  Before I wash this face of mine.

'I will do for my love's sake
  What other lovers would not repair;
Seven years shall come and go
  Before I comb down my yellow hair.

'I'll do more for my love's sake,
  What other lovers will not do;
Seven years shall come and go
  Before I cast off stocking and shoe.

'I will do for my love's sake
  What other lovers they will be slack;
Seven years shall come and go
  Before I cast off my robes of black.

'Go make to me a high, high tower,
  Be sure you make it stout and strong,
And on the top put an honour's gate,
  That my love's ghost may go out and in.'

Anon.

The Daemon Lover

'O where hae ye been, my long, long love,
    These seven long years and more?'
'O I'm come to seek my former vows,
    That ye promised me before.'

'Awa' wi' your former vows,' she says,
    'For they will breed but strife;
Awa' wi' your former vows,' she says,
    'For I am become a wife.

'I am married to a ship-carpenter,
    A ship-carpenter he's bound;
I wadna he kenn'd my mind this nicht
    For twice five hundred pound.'

'O fause are the vows o' womankind,
    But fair is their fause bodie:
I wad never hae trodden on Irish ground,
    Were it no for the love o' thee.'

'If I was to leave my husband dear,
    And my wee young son alsua,
O what hae ye to tak' me to,
    If with you I should gae?'

'The ship wherein my love sall sail
    Is glorious to behowd;
The sails sall be o' the finest silk,
    And the mast o' beaten gowd.'

She has taken up her wee young son,
    Kiss'd him baith cheek and chin;
'O fare ye weel, my wee young son,
    For I'll never see you again!'

She has put her foot on gude ship-board
    And on ship-board she has gane,
And the veil that hangit ower her face
    Was a' wi' gowd begane.

She hadna sail'd a league, a league,
    A league but barely twa,
Till she minded on her husband she left
    And her wee young son alsua.

'O haud your tongue o' weeping,' he says,
    'Let a' your follies a-bee;
I'll show where the white lilies grow
    On the banks o' Italie.'

She hadna sail'd a league, a league,
    A league but barely three,
Till grim, grim grew his countenance
    And gurly grew the sea.

'What hills are yon, yon pleasant hills,
    The sun shines sweetly on?'
'O yon are the hills o' Heaven,' he said,
    'Where you will never won.'

'O whaten-a mountain is yon,' she said,
    Sae dreary wi' frost and snae?'
'O yon is the mountain o' Hell,' he said,
    'Where you and I will gae.'

And aye as she turn'd her round about,
    Aye taller he seem'd to be;
Until that the tops o' that gallant ship
    Nae taller were than he.

He strack the top-mast wi' his hand,
  The fore-mast wi' his knee;
And he brake that gallant ship in twain,
  And sank her in the sea.

                                    Anon.

I Gave You My Love

I gave you my love, not just any love
love that burnt into me like a fire,
O my God, woe to her who would give
deep, deep love to another woman's son.

But were you and I to meet on a moor,
with no pillow but the holly tree
since it is wont to be sharp and wounding,
I would put my own love, under your head.

Anon., trans. from Gaelic by Derick Thomson (b. 1921)

Madge Wildfire's Song

Proud Maisie is in the wood,
  Walking so early;
Sweet Robin sits on the bush,
  Singing so rarely.

'Tell me, thou bonny bird,
  When shall I marry me?'
'When six braw gentlemen
  Kirkward shall carry ye.'

'Who makes the bridal bed,
  Birdie, say truly?'
'The grey-headed sexton
  That delves the grave duly.

'The glow-worm o'er grave and stone
  Shall light thee steady.
The owl from the steeple sing,
  "Welcome, proud lady".'

Sir Walter Scott (1771–1832)

Farewells

Poem for a Goodbye

When you go through
My absence, which is all of you,
And clouds, or suns, no more can be my sky,
My one dissembling will be all –
The inclusive lie
Of being this voice, this look, these few feet tall.

The elements which
Made me from our encounter rich
Cannot be uncreated; there is no
Chaos whose informality
Can cancel, so,
The ritual of your presence, even gone away.

You, then and I
Will masquerade a lie
Diminishing ourselves to be what can
Seem one without the other, while
A greater man,
In hiding, lies behind this look, this smile.

It's he who will
Across sad oceans meet you still,
Startling your carelessness with what once was.
His voice from this past hour will speak,
Cancelling Time's laws:
In the world's presence his hand will touch your cheek.

Foreign can be
Only that sound to you and me.
There is no thought that in its dying goes
Through such a region we do not
In it compose
Each other's selves, each in the other's thought.

187

You leave behind
More than I was, and with a kind
Of sad prevarication take with you
More than I'll be till that day when
Nothing's to do
But say, 'At last', and we are home again.

Norman MacCaig (b. 1910)

The Land o' the Leal

I'm wearin' awa', John,
Like snaw-wreaths in thaw, John,
I'm wearin' awa'
   To the land o' the leal.
There's nae sorrow there, John,
There's neither cauld nor care, John,
The day is aye fair
   In the land o' the leal.

Our bonnie bairn's there, John,
She was baith gude and fair, John,
And oh! we grudged her sair
   To the land o' the leal.
But sorrow's sel' wears past, John,
And joy is a-comin' fast, John,
The joy that's aye to last
   In the land o' the leal.

Sae dear's that joy was bought, John,
Sae free the battle fought, John,

leal = loyal, true

188

That sinfu' man e'er brought
   To the land o' the leal.
O dry your glist'nin' e'e, John,
My saul langs to be free, John,
And angels beckon me
   To the land o' the leal.

Oh! haud ye leal an' true, John,
Your day it's wearin' thro', John,
And I'll welcome you
   To the land o' the leal.
Now fare ye weel, my ain John,
This warld's cares are vain, John,
We'll meet, and we'll be fain,
   In the land o' the leal.

Carolina Oliphant, Lady Nairne (1766–1845)

Fairweill

Allace depairting, grund of wo,
Thou art of everilk joy ane end!
How suld I pairte my lady fro?
How suld I tak my leif to wend?
Sen fals Fortoun is nocht my frend,
Bot evir castis me to keill,
Now sen I most no langir lend,
I tak my leif aganis my will.

to keill = on my back   lend = abide

Fairweill, fairweill, my weillfair may;
Fairweill, fegour most fresche of hew;
Fairweill, the saiffar of assay;
Fairweill, the hart of whyt and blew;
Fairweill, baith kynd, curtas and trew;
Fairweill, woman withowttin ill;
Fairweill, the cumliest that evir I knew.
I tak my leif aganis my will.

Fairweill, my rycht fair lady deir;
Fairweill most wys and womanlie;
Fairweill, my lufe fro yeir to yeir;
Fairweill, thow beriall blycht of blie;
Fairweill, leill lady liberall and free;
Fairweill, that may me saif and spill;
However I fair, go fair weill ye;
I tak my leif aganis my will.

Fairweill fra me, my gudly grace;
Fairweill, the well of wirdines;
Fairweill, my confort in everilk place;
Fairweill, the hoip of steidfastnes;
Fairweill, the rut of my distres;
Fairweill, the luffar trew and still;
Fairweill, the nureis of gentilnes;
I tak my leif aganis my will.

Anon. (sixteenth century)

may = maid	blycht = dazzling
fegour = figure	blie = colour
saiffar = sapphire	spill = destroy
beriall = beryl	wirdines = worthiness

Bonie Lesley

O saw ye bonie Lesley,
   As she gaed o'er the Border?
She's gane, like Alexander,
   To spread her conquests farther.

To see her is to love her,
   And love but her for ever;
For Nature made her what she is,
   And never made anither.

Thou art a queen, fair Lesley –
   Thy subjects, we before thee.
Thou art divine, fair Lesley –
   The hearts o' men adore thee.

The Deil he could na skaith thee,
   Or aught that wad belang thee:
He'd look into thy bonie face,
   And say: –'I canna wrang thee!'

The Powers aboon will tent thee,
   Misfortune sha' na steer thee;
Thou'rt like themsels sae lovely,
   That ill they'll ne'er let near thee.

Return again, fair Lesley,
   Return to Caledonie!
That we may brag we hae a lass
   There's nane again sae bonie.

Robert Burns (1759–96)

from Gilderoy

The last, the fatal hour is come,
    That bears my love from me:
I hear the dead note of the drum,
    I mark the gallows tree!

The bell has toll'd; it shakes my heart;
    The trumpet speaks thy name;
And must my Gilderoy depart,
    To bear a death of shame?

No bosom trembles for thy doom;
    No mourner wipes a tear
The gallows' foot is all thy tomb,
    The sledge is all thy bier.

Oh, Gilderoy! bethought we then
    So soon, so sad, to part,
When first, in Roslin's lovely glen,
    You triumph'd o'er my heart?

Your locks they glitter'd to the sheen,
    Your hunter garb was trim;
And graceful was the ribbon green
    That bound your manly limb!

Ah! little thought I to deplore
    Those limbs in fetters bound;
Or hear, upon thy scaffold floor,
    The midnight hammer sound ...

Thomas Campbell (1777–1844)

Love Lost

The Shepherd's Dochter

Lay her and lea her here i the gantan grund,
  the blythest, bonniest lass o the countryside,
  crined in a timber sark, hapt wi the pride
o hothous flouers, the dearest that could be fund.

Her faither and brithers stand, as suddentlie stunned
  wi the wecht o dule; douce neebours side by side
  wreist and fidge, sclent-luikan, sweirt tae bide
while the Minister's duin and his threep gane wir the wind.

The murners skail, thankfu tae lea thon place
  whar the blythest, bonniest lass liggs in the mouls,
    Lent lilies lowp and cypresses stand stieve,
    Time tae gae back tae the darg, machines and tools
    and beasts and seeds, the things men uis tae live,
and lea the puir lass there in her state o Grace.

Douglas Young (1913–73)

from Ane Metaphoricall Invention of a Tragedie Called Phoenix

For I complaine not of sic common cace,
Which diversely by divers means dois fall:
But I lament my Phoenix rare, whose race,
Whose kynde, whose kin, whose offspring, they be all
In her alone, whome I the Phoenix call.
That fowle which only one at onis did live,
Not lives, alas! though I her praise revive.

And thow (o reuthles Death) sould thow devore
Her? who not only passed by all mens mynde
All other fowlis in hewe, and shape, but more
In rarenes (sen there was none of her kynde
But she alone) whome with thy stounds thow pynde:
And at the last, heth perced her through the heart,
But reuth or pitie, with thy mortall dart.

Yet worst of all, she lived not half her age.
Why stayde thou Tyme at least, which all dois teare
To worke with her? O what a cruell rage,
To cut her off, before her threid did weare!
Wherein all Planets keeps their course, that yeare
It was not by the half yet worne away,
Which sould with her have ended on a day.

King James VI (1566–1625)

The Gentle Ambush

No fabulous warrior came hunting
For your life. Whatever scythed you
Down wore no emblematic garb
Nor magically spirited you away
Through solid wall, stone, wood or glass,
And left a rough replica
When your flesh and blood alive
Became an effigy of clay.
Nothing came: all was in the leaving.
And no ghost haunts the rooms
Your presence filled. What quickens
A half recognition on the stairs
That creak, in the suit holding yet

Your shape, or in the roses
That you hadn't time to prune –
The gentle ambush I'm helpless to resist –
Is: no one's there. And absence
Stares me blankly in the face.

George Macadam (b. 1932)

The Lament of the Border Widow

My love he built me a bonny bower,
And clad it a' wi' lilye flour;
A brawer bower ye ne'er did see,
Than my true love he built for me.

There came a man, by middle day,
He spied his sport, and went away;
And brought the King that very night,
Who brake my bower, and slew my knight.

He slew my knight, to me sae dear;
He slew my knight, and poin'd his gear;
My servants all for life did flee,
And left me in extremitie.

I sew'd his sheet, making my mane;
I watch'd the corpse, myself alane;
I watch'd his body, night and day;
No living creature came that way.

poin'd = made forfeit

197

I took his body on my back,
And whiles I gaed, and whiles I sat;
I digg'd a grave, and laid him in,
And happ'd him with the sod sae green.

But think na ye my heart was sair,
When I laid the moul' on his yellow hair?
O think na ye my heart was wae,
When I turn'd about, away to gae?

Nae living man I'll love again,
Since that my lovely knight is slain;
Wi' ae lock of his yellow hair
I'll chain my heart for evermair.

Anon.

Empty Vessel

I met ayont the cairney
A lass wi' tousie hair
Singin' till a bairnie
That was nae langer there.

Wunds wi warlds to swing
Dinna sing sae sweet,
The licht that bends owre a' thing
Is less ta'en up wi't.

Hugh MacDiarmid (1892–1978)

You Went Away

Suddenly, in my world of you,
You created time.
I walked about in its bitter lanes
Looking for whom I'd lost, afraid to go home.

You stole yourself and gave me this
Torturer for my friend
Who shows me gardens rotting in air
And tells me what I no longer understand.

The birds sing still in the apple trees,
But not in mine. I hear
Only the clock whose wintry strokes
Say, 'Now is now', the same lie over and over.

If I could kill this poem, sticking
My thin pen through its throat,
It would stand crying by your bed
And haunt your cruelty every empty night.

Norman MacCaig (b. 1910)

The Absent One

Wherever I may be
In the woods or in the fields
Whatever the hour of day
Be it dawn or the eventide
My heart still feels it yet
The eternal regret.

199

As I sink into my sleep
The absent one is near
Alone upon my couch
I feel his beloved touch
In work or in repose
We are forever close.

Mary, Queen of Scots (1542–87)
trans. from French by Antonia Fraser

The Shell

Since the shell came and took you in its arms
    Whose body was fine bone
That walked in light beside a place of flowers,
    Why should your son
Years after the eclipse of those alarms
    Perplex this bitten stone
For some spent issue of the sea? Not one
Blue drop of drying blood I could call ours

In all that ocean that you were remains
    To move again. I come
Through darkness from a distance to your tomb
    And feel the swell
Where a dark flood goes headlong to the drains.
    I hear black hailstones drum
Like cold slugs on your skin. There is no bell
To tell what drowned king founders. Violets bloom

Where someone died. I dream that overhead
    I hear a bomber drone

And feel again stiff pumping of slow guns
   Then the All Clear's
Voice break, and the long summing of the dead
   Below the siren's moan
Subdue the salt flood of all blood and tears
To a prolonged strained weeping sound that stuns.

I turn in anger. By whatever stars
   Clear out of drifting rack
This winter evening I revive my claim
   To what has gone
Beyond your dying fall. Through these cold bars
   I feel your breaking back
And live again your body falling on
That flood of stone where no white Saviour came

On Christian feet to lift you to the verge
   Or swans with wings of fire
Whose necks were arched in mourning. Black as coal
   I turn to go
Out of the graveyard. Headstone shadows merge
   And blur. I see the spire
Lift over corpses. And I sense the flow
Of death like honey to make all things whole.

              George MacBeth (b. 1932)

Ae Fond Kiss

   Ae fond kiss, and when we sever, –
   Ae fareweel, and then – for ever!
   Deep in heart-wrung tears I'll pledge thee!
   Warring sighs and groans I'll wage thee!

Who shall say that fortune grieves him,
While the star of hope she leaves him?
Me, nae cheerfu' twinkle lights me, –
Dark despair around benights me.

I'll ne'er blame my partial fancy,
Naething could resist my Nancy;
But to see her was to love her –
Love but her, and love for ever.

Had we never lov'd sae kindly –
Had we never lov'd sae blindly –
Never met – or never parted,
We had ne'er been broken-hearted!

Fare-thee-weel, thou first and fairest!
Fare-thee-weel, thou best and dearest!
Thine be ilka joy and treasure,
Peace, Enjoyment, Love, and Pleasure!

Ae fond kiss, and then we sever!
Ae fareweel, alas! for ever!
Deep in heart-wrung tears I'll pledge thee!
Warring sighs and groans I'll wage thee!

Robert Burns (1759–96)

Lost Love

Who wins his love shall lose her,
Who loses her shall gain,
For still the spirit woos her,
A soul without a stain;

And memory still pursues her
  With longings not in vain!

He loses her who gains her,
  Who watches day by day
The dust of time that stains her,
  The griefs that leave her gray –
The flesh that yet enchains her
  Whose grace hath passed away!

Oh, happier he who gains not
  The love some seem to gain:
The joy that custom stains not
  Shall still with him remain;
The loveliness that wanes not,
  The love that ne'er can wane.

In dreams she grows not older
  The lands of dream among;
Though all the world wax colder,
  Though all the songs be sung,
In dreams doth he behold her
  Still fair and kind and young.

Andrew Lang (1844–1912)

Love in Abeyance

So, We'll Go No More a Roving

So, we'll go no more a roving
    So late into the night,
Though the heart be still as loving,
    And the moon be still as bright.

For the sword outwears its sheath,
    And the soul wears out the breast,
And the heart must pause to breathe,
    And love itself have rest.

Though the night was made for loving,
    And the day returns too soon,
Yet we'll go no more a roving
    By the light of the moon.

George Gordon, Lord Byron (1788–1824)

Wheesht, Wheesht

Wheesht, wheesht, my foolish hert,
For weel ye ken
I widna ha'e ye stert
Auld ploys again.

It's guid to see her lie
Sae snod an' cool,
A' lust o' lovin' by –
Wheesht, wheesht, ye fule!

Hugh MacDiarmid (1892–1978)

207

Returne Thee, Hairt

Returne thee, hairt, hamewart agane,
   And byd whair thou was wont to be;
Thou art ane fule to suffer pane
   For luve of hir that luvis not thee.
   My hairt lat be sic fantesie;
Luve nane bot as they mak thee causs;
   And lat hir seik ane hairt for thee,
For feind a crum of thee scho fawis.

To what effect sowld thow be thrall
   But thank, sen thou hes thy free will?
My hairt, be not sa bestiall,
   Bot knaw who dois thee guid or ill;
   Remane with me and tary still,
And see wha playis best thair pawis,
   And lat fillok ga fling hir fill,
For feind a crum of thee scho fawis.

Thocht scho be fair I will not fenyie;
   Scho is the kind of uthiris ma;
For why thair is a fellone menyie,
   That semis gud, and ar not sa.
   My hairt, tak nowdir pane nor wa,
For Meg, for Meriory, or yit Mawis,
   Bot be thou glaid and latt hir ga,
For feind a crum of thee scho fawis.

feind a crum = not a bit   kind = lover
fawis = gets   uthiris ma = many others
but thank = without thanks   fellone = evil
thair pawis = their own part   menyie = company
fillok = wanton girl   wa = woe
fenyie = feign

208

Becaus I find scho tuik in ill,
    At hir departing thou mak na cair;
Bot all begyld, go whair scho will,
    Beschrew the hairt that mane makis mair.
    My hert, be mirry lait and air,
This is the fynall end and clauss,
    And latt hir fallow ane filly fair,
For feind a crum of thee scho fawis.

           Alexander Scott (?1520–?1590)

beschrew = curse   filly fair = foolish dandy
air = early

My Mind to Me a Kingdom Is

My mind to me a kingdom is
And oh to live there would be bliss!
Why must I sally forth to war
To make my territories the more?
No cosier kingdom ever was,
No war would also mean no loss
My mind to me a kingdom is
And oh to live there will be bliss!

My mind to me a prison is
I must, I must escape from this
I dread the girders of the known
Those bars through which my hopes are flown
The chains of limitation rattle
As once I heard the sounds of battle
My mind to me a prison is
I will, I will escape from this ...

My mind to me a kingdom is
But I will seek there no more bliss:
I'll aim for pleasures in the sky
And you will trust my heart to fly
Forget the solace I once found
In contemplating conquered ground
My mind to me a kingdom was
But now to leave it is no loss.

Antonia Fraser (b. 1932)

Today

saw the last of my Spanish shampoo
lasted an age now that sharing with you
Such a thing of the past is. Giant size
our brand was always a compromise.
My new one's 'tailored exactly to my needs'
nonspill protein rich feeds
body promises to solve my problem hair.
Sweetheart, these days I cannot care

but oh – oh insomniac moonlight
how unhoneyed is my middle of the night.
Oh I can see
you far enough beyond me
how we'll get back together.
Campsites in Spain moonlight heavy weather
Today saw the end of my Spanish shampoo
        the end of my third month without you.

Liz Lochhead (b. 1947)

Wuid-reek

The wuid-reek mells wi the winter haar
And aa the birds are gane;
They're burnan the leaves, the treen are bare,
December rules a dour domain.

The wuid-reek draws a memorie
Frae some far neuk in the brain
When I was a loun and hadna loed
And never kent the world's bane.

Och, burn the leaves and burn the branch
And burn the holly treen!
O winter, burn the hairt I want—
And syne burn mine again!

Sydney Goodsir Smith (1915–75)

The Sleeper

Gazing down upon you I am made aware
Of your lost childhood; ere the grown years
Had brought me to wake your womanliness
Sleeping in beauty. How often thus had you lain
With one arm careless on the counterpane
And one curved back amongst your hair.
Innocence still lingers in the curl of a tress,
And in the little drooping mouth, and the cheek
Puffed up by the pillow. I could shed tears
Knowing that you must awake to endure
The conflict of the flesh in daily stress
Of wasting experiences; and yet my fears

211

Were greater thinking you might not awake.
Through what quiet continents of your own
Are you now walking, and with whom for a friend?
How often am I forgot when you are alone
Standing upon that ultimate verge of consciousness
Which sheers to death: each is alone at the end
And wearied of all this challengeable world
Ready to droop into oblivion
Like a sleepy child: thus, seeing your warm cheek
Pillowed so childlike I fain would bend
To kiss it but pity rebukes me.
Why should I hurry you back from yourself
Out of your own created kingdom:
And yet, and yet, I stoop to your ear and speak
My name in whispers: I who can see
You sleeping serene in your own loneliness
And made aware of myself standing here
Within a loneliness more lone than sleep.

William Soutar (1898–1943)

Change and
Paradox

Ettrick

When we first rade down Ettrick,
Our bridles were ringing, our hearts were dancing,
The waters were singing, the sun was glancing,
An' blithely our hearts rang out thegither,
As we brushed the dew frae the blooming heather,
When we first rade down Ettrick.

When we next rade down Ettrick
The day was dying, the wild birds calling,
The wind was sighing, the leaves were falling,
An' silent an' weary, but closer thegither,
We urged our steeds thro' the faded heather,
     When we next rade down Ettrick.

When I last rade down Ettrick,
The winds were shifting, the storm was waking,
The snow was drifting, my heart was breaking,
For we never again were to ride thegither
In sun or storm on the mountain heather,
     When I last rade down Ettrick.

          Lady John Scott (1810–1900)

from The Testament of Cresseid

Wha wait if all that Chauceir wrait was trew?
Nor I wait nocht if this narratioun
Be authoreist, or fenyeit of the new
Be sum Poeit, threw his Inventioun,

wait = knows   fenyeit of the new = newly invented

Maid to report the Lamentatioun
And wofull end of this lustie Creisseid,
And what distres scho thoillit, and what deid.

When Diomeid had all his appetyte,
And mair, fulfillit of this fair Ladie,
Upon ane uther he set his haill delyte
And send to hir ane Lybell of repudie,
And hir excludit fra his companie.
Than desolait scho walkit up and doun,
And sum men sayis into the Court commoun.

O fair Creisseid, the flour and A per se
Of Troy and Grece, how was thou fortunait!
To change in filth all thy Femininitie,
And be with fleschlie lust sa maculait,
And go amang the Greikis air and lait
Sa giglotlike, takand thy foull plesance!
I have pietie thou suld fall sic mischance.

. . . . .

The Complaint of Cresseid

'O sop of sorrow, sonkin into cair:
O Cative Creisseid, for now and ever mair,
Gane is thy Joy and all thy mirth in Eird,
Of all blyithnes now art thou blaiknit bair.
Thair is na Salve may saif thee of thy sair,
Fell is thy Fortoun, wickit is thy weird:

thoillit = endured   Cative = wretched
air = early   blaiknit = blackened
giglotlike = wantonly

216

Thy blys is baneist, and thy baill on breird;
Under the Eirth, God if I gravin wer,
Whair nane of Grece nor yit of Troy micht heird.

'Whair is thy Chalmer wantounlie besene?
With burely bed and bankouris browderit bene,
Spycis and Wyne to thy Collatioun,
The Cowpis all of gold and silver schene:
The sweit Meitis, servit in plaittis clene,
With Saipheron sals of ane gud sessoun:
Thy gay garmentis with mony gudely Goun,
Thy plesand Lawn pinnit with goldin prene:
All is areir, thy greit Royall Renoun.'

Robert Henryson (c. 1420–c. 1490)

baill on breird = woe burgeoning   schene = bright
wantounlie = gaily   sals = sauce
besene = bedecked   sessoun = seasoning
burely = handsome   prene = pin
bankouris = tapestries   areir = behind, gone
browderit bene = embroidered well

The Figures on the Frieze

Darkness wears off and, dawning into daylight,
they find themselves unmagically together.
He sees the stains of morning in her face.
She shivers, distant in his bitter weather.

Diminishing of legend sets him brooding.
Great goddess-figures conjured from his book
blur what he sees with bafflement of wishing.
Sulky, she feels his fierce, accusing look.

Familiar as her own, his body's landscape
seems harsh and dull to her habitual eyes.
Mystery leaves and, mercilessly flying,
the blind fiends come, emboldened by her cries.

Avoiding simple reach of hand for hand
(which would surrender pride), by noon they stand
withdrawn from touch, reproachfully alone,
small in each other's eyes, tall in their own.

Wild with their misery, they entangle now
in baffling agonies of why and how.
Afternoon glimmers, and they wound anew,
flesh, nerve, bone, gristle in each other's view.

'What have you done to me?' From each proud heart,
new phantoms loom in the deceiving air.
As the light fails, each is consumed apart,
he by his ogre vision, she by her fire.

When night falls, out of a despair of daylight,
they strike the lying attitudes of love,
and through the perturbations of their bodies,
each feels the amazing, murderous legends move.

Alastair Reid (b. 1926)

I Saw the Light Yesterday

I saw the light yesterday.
A long time ago I saw him
when he bathed in the spring.
Summer came, berries sang, he loved me.
Autumn went, the season stole him
withering my heart
And in winter's white cold
I died.
I saw the light yesterday.

Galina V. Ogilvie-Laing (b. 1946)

A Big Hat or What?

It rains
you knot that goddam gawdy
scarf around your white throat.

Time was
I would tell you – take that
bloody scarf off – what the hell if

it rains
you get wet – I like you like
that – all damp and in your pakamac.

What if
the sky fell chicken-licken – what
would you wear then – a big hat or what?

Pete Morgan (b. 1939)

Love Poem 3

Thinking of you
thinking of a bird
that is tied
by the appearance of the seasons.
Thinking of you
on my migration
of all the songs
that are in our spring.
Thinking suddenly
that I may be embarrassed
to say this to you
that we may be becoming
too familiar strangers,
that we may have forgotten
how far we came to be here.

Laughton Johnston (b. 1940)

Paradox

Let us for this love
commit no crime,
not destroy others,
be calm in time
and let our love assume
the varied shapes it finds,
in its own pace and moments.

Lets have no hiddenness,
no deceitful trysts,
for others wait upon
our promised lives:

We can love more, unmarred,
if we resist;
and yet, my darling,
I am unconvinced.

Tom McGrath (b. 1940)

The Scarlet Woman
(for Alexander McGill)

Black-burnin' shame is your garb, quo' they,
And syne gin you turn your face,
It lowes wi' a reid and laithly flame
That springs frae the evil place.

But noo I ha'e met you and seen for mysel'
Your face is the rare reid dawn,
And velvets o' nicht are the gouns you wear
To win the hert o' a man.

And a flame that springs frae the evil place,
And a flame that springs frae Heaven,
Are but as the thocht o' a man maun mak'
As his hert is richt or riven.

221

And glad I am that your face to me
Is the dawn, and no' dreadour,
Nor black affront but the bien nicht haps
Your bonnie form attour.

O burnin' rose o' the love o' God,
Pitch-darkness o' His will,
To Day and to Night, to Life and to Daith,
I gi'e me and fear nae ill.

Hugh MacDiarmid (1892–1978)

A Cold Snap

Something has snapped.
Could it be the chemical bond between
sugar and spice and all things nice?
Something has occurred to me,
that I haven't run into you lately/
That still waters don't run deep either
              they're in chunks/
That I've been saving up for a rainy day
              in a week of sleet/
that you led me up the garden path/
that winter may already have you too
              in its grip/
that you don't grow on trees
              any more than money/
that I've lost even the path
              in the garden/
that everything snapped
              this minute when I saw you:

222

distant as a street photographer's target/
distant as a smile on a billboard/
distant as flowers in a winter's garden/
distant as Mao's era of a thousand blooms/
distant as Cuba and India/
for which sugar and spice too
are so absurdly homesick.

Robert Tait (b. 1943)

Old Loves

There Was a Sang

There was a sang
That aye I wad be singin';
There was a star,
An' clear it used tae shine;
An' liltin' in the starlight
Thro' the shadows
I gaed lang syne.

There was a sang;
But noo, I canna mind it,
There was a star;
But noo, it disna shine.
There was a luve that led me
Thro' the shadows –
And it *was* mine.

Helen B. Cruickshank (1886–1975)

A Former Love

She grew from the crowd,
stepping, streaming along the pavement,
head tossed high,
hair longer than before.
She saw me,
swooped head to breast,
rushed past.

A scent hung in the air.

Giles Gordon (b. 1940)

227

O Joy of Love's Renewing

O joy of love's renewing,
    Could love be born again;
Relenting for thy rueing,
    And pitying my pain:
O joy of love's awaking,
    Could love arise from sleep,
Forgiving our forsaking
    The fields we would not reap!

Fleet, fleet we fly, pursuing
    The love that fled amain,
But will he list our wooing,
    Or call we but in vain?
Ah! vain is all our wooing,
    And all our prayers are vain,
Love listeth not our suing,
    Love will not wake again.

Andrew Lang (1844–1912)

Once Fondly Lov'd

Once fondly lov'd, and still remember'd dear,
    Sweet early object of my youthful vows,
Accept this mark of friendship, warm, sincere –
    Friendship! 'tis all cold duty now allows: –

And when you read the simple, artless rhymes,
    One friendly sigh for him – he asks no more –
Who distant burns in flaming torrid climes,
    Or haply lies beneath th' Atlantic roar.

                              Robert Burns (1759–96)

The Loch Ness Monster

Sometimes at night when the wind blows hard
the Loch Ness monster is lonely
for his extinct contemporaries
the warm flying fox and the luscious algae

so too in the long silent hours when the wind blows
(the black water closing over my head)
I am lonely for you my extinct love
pinioned down there in the strata

'I love you' I cry –
but you cannot weep or move your head

and I am terrified I shall not be near you again
until the rocks are broken
and our dead dust is blown out into space.

                              Tom Buchan (b. 1931)

Kiss'd Yestreen

Kiss'd yestreen, and kiss'd yestreen,
Up the Gallowgate, down the Green:
I've woo'd wi' lords, and woo'd wi' lairds,
I've mool'd wi' carles and mell'd wi' cairds,
I've kiss'd wi' priests – 'twas done i' the dark,
Twice in my gown and thrice in my sark;
But priest, nor lord, nor loon can gie
Sic kindly kisses as he gae me.

Anon.

mool'd = played   mell'd = meddled
sark = shirt

Farewell

We were gone from each other
not that I was happy
in this country
nor not happy
when your chair was empty

which you had filled (rounded)
not as a theory
but as a fruit ripening
ripening towards harvest

in another country
where some evening you'll see
in another chair
by your autumn nursery

a sky barred and ruled
with a red cloud above
and perhaps think of me
late late in that world
where your round cornstacks are.

Iain Crichton Smith (b. 1928)

Corn Riggs

It was upon a Lammas night,
    When corn rigs are bonie,
Beneath the moon's unclouded light
    I held awa to Annie:
The time flew by, wi' tentless heed,
    Till 'tween the late and early;
Wi' sma' persuasion she agreed,
    To see me thro' the barley.

    Corn rigs, an' barley rigs,
        An' corn rigs are bonie:
    O, I'll ne'er forget that happy night,
        Amang the rigs wi' Annie.

The sky was blue, the wind was still,
    The moon was shining clearly;
I set her down, wi' right good will,
    Amang the rigs o' barley:
I ken't her heart was a' my ain;
    I lov'd her most sincerely;
I kiss'd her owre and owre again,
    Amang the rigs o' barley.

231

I lock'd her in my fond embrace;
  Her heart was beating rarely:
My blessings on that happy place,
  Amang the rigs o' barley!
But by the moon and stars so bright,
  That shone that night so clearly!
She ay shall bless that happy night,
  Amang the rigs o' barley.

I hae been blythe wi' comrades dear;
  I hae been merry drinking;
I hae been joyfu' gath'rin' gear;
  I hae been happy thinking:
But a' the pleasures e'er I saw,
  Tho' three times doubl'd fairly,
That happy night was worth them a',
  Amang the rigs o' barley.

Robert Burns (1759–96)

Enduring Love

The Commemoration

I wish I could proclaim
My faith enshrined in you
And spread among a few
Our high but hidden fame,
That we new life have spun
Past all that's thought and done,
And someone or no one
Might tell both did the same.

Material things will pass
And we have seen the flower
And the slow falling tower
Lie gently in the grass,
But meantime we have stored
Riches past bed and board
And nursed another hoard
Than callow lad and lass.

Invisible virtue now
Expands upon the air
Although no fruit appear
Nor weight bend down the bough,
And harvests truly grown
For someone or no one
Are stored and safely won
In hollow heart and brow.

How can one thing remain
Except the invisible,
The echo of a bell
Long rusted in the rain?
This strand we weave into
Our monologue of two,

And time cannot undo
That strong and subtle chain.

Edwin Muir (1887–1959)

The Confirmation

Yes, yours, my love, is the right human face.
I in my mind had waited for this long,
Seeing the false and searching for the true,
Then found you as a traveller finds a place
Of welcome suddenly amid the wrong
Valleys and rocks and twisting roads. But you,
What shall I call you? A fountain in a waste,
A well of water in a country dry,
Or anything that's honest and good, an eye
That makes the whole world bright. Your open heart,
Simple with giving, gives the primal deed,
The first good world, the blossom, the blowing seed,
The hearth, the steadfast land, the wandering sea,
Not beautiful or rare in every part,
But like yourself, as they were meant to be.

Edwin Muir (1887–1959)

from To His Mistress

My dear and only Love, I pray
    This noble World of thee,
Be govern'd by no other Sway
    But purest Monarchie.
For if Confusion have a Part,
    Which vertuous Souls abhore,
And hold a Synod in thy Heart,
    I'll never love thee more.

Like *Alexander* I will reign,
    And I will reign alone,
My Thoughts shall evermore disdain
    A Rival on my Throne.
He either fears his Fate too much,
    Or his Deserts are small,
That puts it not unto the Touch,
    To win or lose it all.

James Graham, Marquis of Montrose (1612–50)

Swans

Here come two swans below the Roman bridge,
Mirrored images of innocence in a divided unity,
Swimming in their unapproachable regality:
They idle down through Eskside
To Goose Green, decking and reaching
With consequential preen;
And the bottom of the river holds
A magic fascination that draws their

Deep attention, then with brisk decision,
They strike again through the water
On a ripple of atoms.

On this summer-laden and domestic stream
They seem to compass more than a common share
Of time, as if each movement on the river
Was through a gateway into an eternity
Peculiar to swans:
Here four-footed sensuality may appear far remote
From this ideal pair;
They have an air of delicate certainty,
An instinct awareness and assurance
That is tender like a loving caress.

Those night-star eyes can look on far countries
Through the vast black night of the world,
And, by mere looking, they light the dark
Of our day with instant revelation.
These swans are like deep-sea fishermen
Who know the constant lure of ocean sprays,
And are all the time aware
Of immense uncharted continents within.

In exquisite form, male and female, created
He them: they move dreamlike in our
World, while we think mundanely in theirs;
Yet our visions are parallel, beneath the white down
The strong pulse beats that echoes along
The red-river flood of our hearts:
And in our long summer bliss
There is no foreseeable, and sullen,
Term to our living joy.

Morley Jamieson (b. 1917)

Words, for E

The sky is blue, or something. Anyway, it's there.
Your words are hands, stroking me, stroking the sky,
Blue sky, names, people. It's marvellous. I'm king,
And your words are a line of ships. The guns fire.
Blue sky, names, people. I take the salute.

You are beautiful, sometimes. Now.
I feel for words for you. The ship rising, falling,
The horizon, a line rising, falling, behind your hair.
Words rise, spray. I like to think of you as giving
Structure. A gentleness. A constancy.

                              Tom Leonard (b. 1944)

Less than Love

We've seen some trees when they are seized by storms
enduring to be greener than before,
or if ill-bent from tall intended forms
then they'll incline to change, accepting more
within the grain their lot each godly day ...
though not in pay of our desires and fears.
There is a hurricane charging its way
through us which no one sees and no one hears.
We hide it well among our leaves. We must.

Sometimes a subtle fiend it seems a friend,
just as a gentle breeze dispels mistrust –
in deed much of its power we expend,
yet if for *love* we do, little is lost.
Less, takes a fee, but love can stand the cost.

Aileen Campbell Nye (b. 1933)

Constant Love in All Conditions

Now doeth disdainfull Saturne sadd and olde
With ycie bearde enjoye his frosen raigne
His hoarie haires and snowie mantle colde
Ou'rcovers hills and everie pleasant plaine
While daez'd with frost, whiles droun'd with rapping raine
Doe beasts and birds bewaile there carefull cace
With longsume lookes in houpe to see againe
Sweet savoured Flora showe her aimeled face.

And looke how long they are in this estate,
This dolent season so there courage dants
That now no Cupide with his golden bate
Darr make there harts his harbour where he hants
Bot rather deade as are the trees and plants,
There spirits of life must hide them at the hart
Wherethrough there kindlie courage daylie scants
Whill mounting Phoebus make them to revert.

And shall I then like bride or beast forgett
For anie stormes that threatning heaven can send
That object sweete, wheron my hart is sett
Whome for to serve my senses all I bend
My inward flame with colde it dothe contend
The more it burnes, the more restrain'd it be
No winters frost, nor summers heate can end
Or staye the course of constant love in me.

King James VI (1566–1625)

John Anderson, My Jo

John Anderson, my jo, John,
When we were first acquent;
Your locks were like the raven,
Your bonie brow was brent;
But now your brow is beld, John,
Your locks are like the snaw;
But blessings on your frosty pow,
John Anderson, my jo!

John Anderson, my jo, John,
We clamb the hill thegither;
And mony a canty day John,
We've had wi' ane anither:
Now we maun totter down, John,
And hand in hand we'll go;
And sleep thegither at the foot,
John Anderson, my jo!

Robert Burns (1759–96)

241

Three Love Poems for My Wife

Touch

and no sound
and no word spoken
and the window pane
grey in dwindling light
and no word spoken
but touch, your touch
upon my hand veined
by the changing years
that gave and took away
yet gave a touch
that took away
the years between
and brought to this grey day
the brightness we had seen
before the years had grown between.

Tower on Cliff Top

When I took your hand, securing
you at the turn of the stone stair,
for the narrow step deepened by unknown
steps that climbed that dark,
(many generations in that dark
that split the day from day)
the sky broke blue above;
below the stone cube, the flat sea,
then in this place we knew
what we had known before
the years grew in us together,

yet never knew as here and now
in sudden glare and roaring airs,
as time had waited on this time
to know this in our broken day
when I took your hand.

Love in Age

Now that we have had our day, you
having carried, borne children,
been responsible through the wearing years,
in this moment and the next
and still the next as our love
spreads to tomorrow's horizon,
we talk a little before silence.

Let the young make up their love songs,
about which subject they are securely ignorant.
Let them look into eyes that mirror
themselves. Let them groan and ululate
their desire into a microphone. Let them
shout their proclamations over the tannoy
– a whisper is enough for us.

George Bruce (b. 1909)

from Evin Dead Behold I Breathe

Evin dead behold I breathe!
My breath procures my pane;
Els dolour, eftir death,
Suld slaik, when I war slane:
Bot destinie's disdane
So span my fatall threid,
Bot mercy, to remane
A martyr, quik and deid.
O fatall deidly feid!
O rigour but remorse!
Since thair is no remeid,
Come patience, perforce.

Yit tyme sall try my treuth,
And panefull patient pairt.
Thoght love suld rage but reuth,
And death with deidly dairt
Suld sey to caus me smart;
Nor fortuns fickill vheill:
All suld not change my hairt,
Whilk is als true as steill.
I am not lyk ane eill;
To slippe, nor yet to slyde.
Love, fortun, death, fairweill
For I am bound to byd.

Alexander Montgomerie (?1545–?1610)

List of Authors and Titles